The New Frontiers of Freedom: From the Alps to the Aegean

E. Alexander Powell

Esprios.com

THE NEW FRONTIERS OF FREEDOM
THE ARMY BEHIND THE ARMY
THE LAST FRONTIER
GENTLEMEN ROVERS
THE END OF THE TRAIL
FIGHTING IN FLANDERS
THE ROAD TO GLORY
VIVE LA FRANCE!
ITALY AT WAR

CHARLES SCRIBNER'S SONS

THE NEW FRONTIERS OF FREEDOM

FROM THE ALPS TO THE ÆGEAN

BY

E. ALEXANDER POWELL

1920

TO A REAL AND LIFELONG FRIEND
MAJOR J. STANLEY MOORE
OF THE DEPARTMENT OF STATE

THE QUEEN OF RUMANIA TELLS MAJOR POWELL THAT SHE
ENJOYS BEING A QUEEN

AN ACKNOWLEDGMENT

Owing to the disturbed conditions which prevailed throughout most of southeastern Europe during the summer and autumn of 1919, the journey recorded in the following pages could not have been taken had it not been for the active cooperation of the Governments through whose territories we traveled and the assistance afforded by their officials and by the officers of their armies and navies, to say nothing of the hospitality shown us by American diplomatic and consular representatives, relief-workers and others. From the Alps to the Ægean, in Italy, Dalmatia, Montenegro, Albania, Macedonia, Turkey, Rumania, Hungary and Serbia we met with universal courtesy and kindness.

For the innumerable courtesies which we were shown in Italy and the regions under Italian occupation I am indebted to His Excellency Francisco Nitti, Prime Minister of Italy, and to former Premier Orlando, to General Armando Diaz, Commander-in-Chief of the Italian Armies; to Lieutenant-General Albricci, Minister of War; to Admiral Thaon di Revel, Minister of Marine; to Vice-Admiral Count Enrice Mulo, Governor-General of Dalmatia; to Lieutenant-General Piacentini, Governor-General of Albania, to Lieutenant-General Montanari, commanding the Italian troops in Dalmatia; to Rear-Admiral Wenceslao Piazza, commanding the Italian forces in the Curzolane Islands; to Lieutenant-Colonel Antonio Chiesa, commanding the Italian troops in Montenegro; to Colonel Aldo Aymonino, Captain Marchese Piero Ricci and Captain Ernesto Tron of the *Comando Supremo*, the last-named being our companion and cicerone on a motor-journey of nearly three thousand miles; to Captain Roggieri of the Royal Italian Navy, Chief of Staff to the Governor-General of Dalmatia; to Captain Amedeo Acton, commanding the *"Filiberto"*; to Captain Fausto M. Leva, commanding the *"Dandolo"*; to Captain Giulio Menin, commanding the *"Puglia,"* and to Captain Filipopo, commanding the *"Ardente,"* all of whom entertained us with the hospitality so characteristic of the Italian Navy; to Lieutenant Giuseppe Castruccio, our cicerone in

Rome and my companion on dirigible and airplane flights; to Lieutenant Bartolomeo Poggi and Engineer-Captain Alexander Ceccarelli, respectively commander and chief engineer of the destroyer "*Sirio*," both of whom, by their unfailing thoughtfulness and courtesy added immeasurably to the interest and enjoyment of our voyage down the Adriatic from Fiume to Valona; to Lieutenant Pellegrini di Tondo, our companion on the long journey by motor across Albania and Macedonia; to Lieutenant Morpurgo, who showed us many kindnesses during our stay in Salonika; to Baron San Martino of the Italian Peace Delegation; to Lieutenant Stroppa-Quaglia, attaché of the Italian Peace Delegation, and, above all else, to those valued friends, Cavaliere Giuseppe Brambilla, Counselor of the Italian Embassy in Washington; Major-General Gugliemotti, Military Attaché, and Professor Vittorio Falorsi, formerly Secretary of the Embassy at Washington, to each of whom I am indebted for countless kindnesses. No list of those to whom I am indebted would be complete, however, unless itincluded the name of my valued and lamented friend, the late Count V. Macchi di Cellere, Italian Ambassador to the United States, whose memory I shall never forget.

I welcome this opportunity of expressing our appreciation of the hospitality shown us by their Majesties King Ferdinand and Queen Marie of Rumania, who entertained us at their Castle of Pelesch, and of acknowledging my indebtedness to His Excellency M. Bratianu, Prime Minister of Rumania, and to M. Constantinescu, Rumanian Minister of Commerce.

I am profoundly appreciative of the honor shown me by His Majesty King Nicholas of Montenegro, and my grateful thanks are also due to His Excellency General A. Gvosdenovitch, Aide-de-Camp to the King and former Minister of Montenegro to the United States.

For the trouble to which they put themselves in facilitating my visit to Jugoslavia I am deeply grateful to His Excellency M. Grouitch, Minister from the Kingdom of the Serbs, Croats and Slovenes to the United States, and to His Excellency M. Vesnitch, the Jugoslav Minister to France.

From the long list of our own country-people abroad to whom we are indebted for hospitality and kindness, I wish particularly to thank the Honorable Thomas Nelson Page, formerly American Ambassador to Italy; the Honorable Percival Dodge, American Minister to the Kingdom of the Serbs, Croats and Slovenes; the Honorable Gabriel Bie Ravndal, American Commissioner and Consul-General in Constantinople; the Honorable Francis B. Keene, American Consul-General in Rome; Colonel Halsey Yates, U.S.A., American Military Attaché at Bucharest; Lieutenant-Colonel L.G. Ament, U.S.A., Director of the American Relief Administration in Rumania, who was our host during our stay in Bucharest, as was Major Carey of the American Red Cross during our visit in Salonika; Dr. Frances Flood, Director of the American Red Cross Hospital in Monastir, and Mrs. Mary Halsey Moran, in charge of American relief work in Constantza, in whose hospitable homes we found a warm welcome during our stays in those cities; Reverend and Mrs. Phineas Kennedy of Koritza, Albania; Dr. Henry King, President of Oberlin College, and Charles R. Crane, Esquire, of the Commission on Mandates in the Near East; Dr. Fisher, Professor of Modern History at Robert College, Constantinople; and finally of three friends in Rome, Mr. Cortese, representative in Italy of the Associated Press; Dr. Webb, founder and director of the hospital for facial wounds at Udine; and Nelson Gay, Esquire, the celebrated historian, all three of whom shamefully neglected their personal affairs in order to give me suggestions and assistance

.To all of those named above, and to many others who are not named, I am deeply grateful.

E. Alexander Powell.

Yokohama, Japan,
February, 1920.

CONTENTS

AN ACKNOWLEDGMENT

CONTENTS

ILLUSTRATIONS

    I. ACROSS THE REDEEMED LANDS

   II. THE BORDERLAND OF SLAV AND LATIN

  III. THE CEMETERY OF FOUR EMPIRES

  IV. UNDER THE CROSS AND THE CRESCENT

   V. WILL THE SICK MAN OF EUROPE RECOVER?

  VI. WHAT THE PEACE-MAKERS HAVE DONE ON THE DANUBE

 VII. MAKING A NATION TO ORDER

ILLUSTRATIONS

The Queen of Rumania tells Major Powell that she enjoys being a Queen

His first sight of the Terra Irridenta

The end of the day

A little mother of the Tyrol

Italy's new frontier

This is not Venice, as you might suppose, but Trieste

At the gates of Fiume

The inhabitants of Fiume cheering d'Annunzio and his raiders

His Majesty Nicholas I, King of Montenegro

Two conspirators of Antivari

The head men of Ljaskoviki, Albania, waiting to bid Major and Mrs. Powell farewell

The ancient walls of Salonika

Yildiz Kiosk, the favorite palace of Abdul-Hamid and his successors on the throne of Osman

The Red Badge of Mercy in the Balkans

The gypsy who demanded five lei for the privilege of taking her picture

A peasant of Old Serbia

King Ferdinand tells Mrs. Powell his opinion of the fashion in which the Peace Conference treated Rumania

The wine-shop which is pointed out to visitors as "the Cradle of the War"

CHAPTER I

ACROSS THE REDEEMED LANDS

It is unwise, generally speaking, to write about countries and peoples when they are in a state of political flux, for what is true at the moment of writing may be misleading the next. But the conditions which prevailed in the lands beyond the Adriatic during the year succeeding the signing of the Armistice were so extraordinary, so picturesque, so wholly without parallel in European history, that they form a sort of epilogue, as it were, to the story of the great conflict. To have witnessed the dismemberment of an empire which was hoary with antiquity when the Republic in which we live was yet unborn; to have seen insignificant states expand almost overnight into powerful nations; to have seen and talked with peoples who did not know from day to day the form of government under which they were living, or the name of their ruler, or the color of their flag; to have seen millions of human beings transferred from sovereignty to sovereignty like cattle which have been sold—these are sights the like of which will probably not be seen again in our times or in those of our children, and, because they serve to illustrate a chapter of History which is of immense importance, I have tried to sketch them, in brief, sharp outline, in this book.

Because I was curious to see for myself how the countrymen of Andreas Hofer in South Tyrol would accept their enforced Italianization; whether the Italians of Fiume would obey the dictum of President Wilson that their city must be Slav; how the Turks of Smyrna and the Bulgarians of Thrace would welcome Hellenic rule; whether the Croats and Slovenes and Bosnians and Montenegrins were content to remain pasted in the Jugoslav stamp-album; and because I wished to travel through these disputed regions while the conditions and problems thus created were still new, we set out, my wife and I, at about the time the Peace Conference was drawing to a close, on a journey, made largely by motor-car and destroyer, which took us from the Adige to the Vardar and from the Vardar to the

The New Frontiers of Freedom: From the Alps to the Aegean

Pruth, along more than five thousand miles of those new national boundaries—drawn in Paris by a lawyer, a doctor and a college professor—which have been termed, with undue optimism perhaps, the frontiers of freedom.

Some of the things which I shall say in these pages will probably give offense to those governments which showed us many courtesies. Those who are privileged to speak for governments are fond of asserting that *their* governments have nothing to conceal and that they welcome honest criticism, but long experience has taught me that when they are told unpalatable truths governments are usually as sensitive and resentful as friends. Now it has always seemed to me that a writer owes his first allegiance to his readers. To misinform them by writing only half-truths for the sake of retaining the good-will of those written about is as unethical, to my way of thinking, as it is for a newspaper to suppress facts which the public is entitled to know in order not to offend its advertisers. Were I to show my appreciation of the many kindnesses which we received from governments, sovereigns and officials by refraining from unfavorable comment on their actions and their policies, this book would possess about as much intrinsic value as those sumptuous volumes which are written to the order of certain Latin-American republics, in which the authors studiously avoid touching on such embarrassing subjects as revolutions, assassinations, earthquakes, finances, or fevers for fear of scaring away foreign investors or depreciating the government securities.

It is entirely possible that in forming some of my conclusions I was unconsciously biased by the hospitality and kindness we were shown, for it is human nature to have a more friendly feeling for the man who invites you to dinner or sends you a card to his club than for the man who ignores your existence; it is probable that I not infrequently placed the wrong interpretation on what I saw and heard, especially in the Balkans; and, in those cases where I have rashly ventured to indulge in prophecy, it is more than likely that future events will show that as a prophet I am not an unqualified success. In spite of these shortcomings, however, I would like my readers to believe that I have made a conscientious effort to place before them, in the following pages, a plain and unprejudiced account of how the essays in map-making of the lawyer, the doctor and the college professor in Paris have affected the peoples, problems and politics of that vast region which stretches from the Alps to the Ægean.

The Queen of the Adriatic never looked more radiantly beautiful than on the July morning when, from the landing-stage in front of the Danieli, we boarded the *vapore* which, after an hour's steaming up the teeming Guidecca and across the outlying lagoons, set us down at the road-head, on the mainland, where young Captain Tron, of the Comando Supremo, was awaiting us with a big gray staff-car. Captain Tron, who had been born on the Riviera and spoke English like an Oxonian, had been aide-de-camp to the Prince of Wales during that young gentleman's prolonged stay on the Italian front. He was selected by the Italian High Command to accompany us, I imagine, because of his ability to give intelligent answers to every conceivable sort of question, his tact, and his unfailing discretion. His chief weakness was his proclivity for road-burning, in which he was enthusiastically abetted by our Sicilian chauffeur, who, before attaining to the dignity of driving a staff-car, had spent an apprenticeship of two years in piloting ammunition-laden *camions* over the narrow and perilous roads which led to the positions held by the Alpini amid the higher peaks, during which he learned to save his tires and his brake-linings by taking on two wheels instead of four the hairpin mountain turns. Now I am perfectly willing to travel as fast as any one, if necessity demands it, but to tear through a region as beautiful as Venetia at sixty miles an hour, with the incomparable landscape whirling past in a confused blur, like a motion-picture film which is being run too fast because the operator is in a hurry to get home, seems to me as unintelligent as it is unnecessary. Like all Italian drivers, moreover, our chauffeur insisted on keeping his cut-out wide open, thereby producing a racket like a machine-gun, which, though it gave warning of our approach when we were still a mile away, made any attempt at conversation, save by shouting, out of the question.

Because I wished to follow Italy's new frontiers from their very beginning, at that point where the boundaries of Italy, Austria and Switzerland meet near the Stelvio Pass, our course from Venice lay northwestward, across the dusty plains of Venetia, shimmering in the summer heat, the low, pleasant-looking villas of white or pink or sometimes pale blue stucco, set far back in blazing gardens, peering coyly out at us from between the ranks of stately cypresses which lined the highway, like daintily-gowned girls seeking an excuse for a flirtation. Dotting the Venetian plain are many quaint and charming towns of whose existence the tourist, traveling by train, never dreams, their massive walls, sometimes defended by moats and draw-bridges, bearing mute witness to this region's stormy and romantic past. Towering above the red-tiled roofs of each of these Venetian plain-towns is its slender campanile, and, as each campanile is of distinctive design, it serves as a landmark by which the town can be identified from afar. Through the narrow, cobble-paved streets of Vicenza we swept, between rows of shops opening into cool, dim, vaulted porticoes, where the townspeople can lounge and stroll and gossip without exposing themselves to rain or sun; through Rovereto, noted for its silk-culture and for its old, old houses, superb examples of the domestic architecture of the Middle Ages, with faded frescoes on their quaint façades; and so up the rather monotonous and uninteresting valley of the Adige until, just as the sun was sinking behind the Adamello, whose snowy flanks were bathed in the rosy *Alpenglow*, we came roaring into Trent, the capital and center of the Trentino, which, together with Trieste and its adjacent territory, composed the regions commonly referred to by Italians before the war as *Italia Irredenta*—Unredeemed Italy.

Rooms had been reserved for us at the Hotel Trento, a famous tourist hostelry in pre-war days, which had been used as headquarters by the field-marshal commanding the Austrian forces in the Trentino, signs of its military occupation being visible in the scratched woodwork and ruined upholstery. The spurs of the Austrian staff officers on duty in Trent, as Major Rupert Hughes once remarked of the American staff officers on duty in Washington, must have been dripping with furniture polish.

Trent—or Trento, as its new owners call it—is a place of some 30,000 inhabitants, built on both banks of the Adige, in the center of a great bowl-shaped valley which is completely hemmed in by towering mountain walls. In the church of Santa Maria Maggiore the celebrated Council of Trent sat in the middle of the sixteenth century for nearly a decade. On the eastern side of the town rises the imposing Castello del Buon Consiglio, once the residence of the Prince-Bishops but now a barracks for Italian soldiery.

No one who knows Trent can question the justice of Italy's claims to the city and to the rich valleys surrounding it, for the history, the traditions, the language, the architecture and the art of this region are as characteristically Italian as though it had never been outside the confines of the kingdom. The system of mild and fertile Alpine valleys which compose the so-called Trentino have an area of about 4,000 square miles and support a population of 380,000 inhabitants, of whom 375,000, according to a census made by the Austrians themselves, are Italian. An enclave between Lombardy and Venetia, a rough triangle with its southern apex at the head of the Lake of Garda, the Trentino, originally settled by Italian colonists who went forth as early as the time of the Roman Republic, was for centuries an independent Italian prince-bishopric, being arbitrarily annexed to Austria upon the fall of Napoleon. In spite of the tyrannical and oppressive measures pursued by the Austrian authorities in their attempts to stamp out the affection of the Trentini for their Italian motherland, in spite of the systematic attempts to Germanicize the region, in spite of the fact that it was an offense punishable by imprisonment to wear the Italian colors, to sing the Italian national hymn, or to have certain Italian books in their possession, the poor peasants of these mountain valleys remained unswervingly loyal to Italy throughout a century of persecution. Little did the thousands of American and British tourists who were wont to make of the Trentino a summer playground, climbing its mountains, fishing in its rivers, motoring over its superb highways, stopping in its great hotels, realize the silent but desperate struggle which was in progress between this handful of Italian exiles and the empire of the Hapsburgs.

The attitude of the Austrian authorities toward their unwilling subjects of the Trentino was characterized by a vindictiveness as savage as it was shortsighted. Like the Germans in Alsace, they made the mistake of thinking that they could secure the loyalty of the people by awing and terrorizing them, whereas these methods had the effect of hardening the determination of the Trentini to rid themselves of Austrian rule. Cæsare Battisti was deputy from Trent to the parliament in Vienna. When war was declared he escaped from Austria and enlisted in the Italian army, precisely as hundreds of American colonists joined the Continental Army upon the outbreak of the Revolution. During the first Austrian offensive he was captured and sentenced to death, being executed while still suffering from his wounds. The fact that the rope parted twice beneath his weight added the final touch to the brutality which marked every stage of the proceeding. The execution of Battista provided a striking object-lesson for the inhabitants of the Trentino and of Italy—but not the sort of object-lesson which the Austrians had intended. Instead of terrifying them, it but fired them in their determination to end that sort of thing forever. From Lombardy to Sicily Battista was acclaimed a hero and a martyr; photographs of him on his way to execution—an erect and dignified figure, a dramatic contrast to the shambling, sullen-faced soldiery who surrounded him—were displayed in every shop-window in the kingdom; all over Italy streets and parks and schools were named to perpetuate his memory.

HIS FIRST SIGHT OF THE TERRA IRRIDENTA
King Victor Emanuel arriving at Trieste on a destroyer after its occupation by the Italians

Had there been in my mind a shadow of doubt as to the justice of Italy's annexation of the Trentino, it would have been dissipated when, after dinner, we stood on the balcony of the hotel in the moonlight, looking down on the great crowd which filled to overflowing the brilliantly lighted piazza. A military band was playing *Garibaldi's Hymn* and the people stood in silence, as in a church, the faces of many of them wet with tears, while the familiar strains, forbidden by the Austrian under penalty of imprisonment, rose triumphantly on the evening air to be echoed by the encircling mountains. At last the exiles had come home. And from his marble pedestal, high above the multitude, the great statue of Dante looked serenely out across the valleys and the mountains which are "unredeemed" no longer.

Though Italy's original claims in this region, as made at the beginning of the war, included only the so-called Trentino (by which is generally meant those Italian-speaking districts which used to belong to the bishopric of Trent) together with those parts of South Tyrol which are in population overwhelmingly Italian, she has since demanded, and by the Peace Conference has been awarded, the territory known as the upper Adige, which comprises all the districts lying within the basin of the Adige and of its tributary, the Isarco, including the cities of Botzen and Meran. By the annexation of this region Italy has pushed her frontier as far north as the Brenner, thereby bringing within her borders upwards of 180,000 German-speaking Tyrolese who have never been Italian in any sense and who bitterly resent being transferred, without their consent and without a plebiscite, to Italian rule.

The Italians defend their annexation of the Upper Adige by asserting that Italy's true northern boundary, in the words of Eugène de Beauharnais, written, when Viceroy of Italy, to his stepfather, Napoleon, "is that traced by Nature on the summits of the mountains, where the waters that flow into the Black Sea are divided from those that flow into the Adriatic." Viewed from a purely geographical standpoint, Italy's contention that the great semi-circular barrier of the Alps forms a natural and clearly defined frontier, separating her by a clean-cut line from the countries to the north, is unquestionably a sound one. Any one who has entered Italy from the north must have instinctively felt, as he reached the summit of this mighty mountain wall and looked down on the warm and fertile slopes sweeping southward to the plains, "Here Italy begins."

Italy further justifies her annexation of the German-speaking Upper Adige on the ground of national security. She must, she insists, possess henceforward a strong and easily defended northern frontier. She is tired of crouching in the valleys while her enemies dominate her from the mountain-tops. Nor do I blame her. Her whole history is punctuated by raids and invasions launched from these northern heights. But the new frontier, in the words of former Premier Orlando, "can be defended by a handful of men, while therefore the defense of the Trentino salient required half the Italian forces, the other half being constantly threatened with envelopment."

As I have already pointed out, the annexation of the Upper Adige means the passing of 180,000 German-speaking Austrians under Italian sovereignty, including the cities of Botzen and Meran; the ancient centers of German-Alpine culture, Brixen and Sterzing; of Schloss Tyrol, which gives the whole country its name; and, above all, of the Parsier valley, the home of Andreas Hofer, whose life and living memory provide the same inspiration for the Germans of Tyrol that the exploits and traditions of Garibaldi do for the Italians.

That Italy is not insensible to the perils of bringing within her borders a *bloc* of people who are not and never will be Italian, is clearly shown by the following extract from an Italian official publication:

"In claiming the Upper Adige, Italy does not forget that the highest valleys are inhabited by 180,000 Germans, a residuum from the immigration in the Middle Ages. It is not a problem to be taken lightheartedly, but it is impossible for Italy to limit herself only to the Trentino, as that would not give her a satisfactory military frontier. From that point of view, the basin of Bolzano (Bozen) is as strictly necessary to Italy as the Rhine is to France."

The New Frontiers of Freedom: From the Alps to the Aegean

THE END OF THE DAY
A Tyrolean peasant woman returning from the fields

No one has been more zealous in the cause of Italy than I have been; no one has been more whole-heartedly with the Italians in their splendid efforts to recover the lands to which they are justly entitled; no one more thoroughly realizes the agonies of apprehension which Italy has suffered from the insecurity of her northern borders, or has been more keenly alive to the grim but silent struggle which has been waged between her statesmen and her soldiers as to whether the broad statesmanship which aims at international good-feeling and abstract justice, or the narrower and more selfish policy dictated by military necessity, should govern the delimitation of her new frontiers. But, because I am a friend of Italy, and because I wish her well, I view with grave misgivings the wisdom of thus creating, within her own borders, a new *terra irredenta*; I question the quality of statesmanship which insists on including within the Italian body politic an alien and irreconcilable minority which will probably always be a latent source of trouble, one which may, as the result of some unforseen irritation, break into an open sore. It would seem to me that Italy, in annexing the Upper Adige, is storing up for herself precisely the same troubles which Austria did when she held against their will the Italians of the Trentino, or as Germany did when, in order to give herself a strategic frontier, she annexed Alsace and Lorraine. When Italy puts forward the argument that she must hold everything up to the Brenner because of her fear of invasion by the puny and bankrupt little state which is all that is left of the Austrian Empire, she is but weakening her case. Her soundest excuse for the annexation of this region lies in her fear that a reconstituted and revengeful Germany might some day use the Tyrol as a gateway through which to launch new armies of invasion and conquest. But, no matter what her friends may think of the wisdom or justice of Italy's course, her annexation of the Upper Adige is a *fait accompli* which is not likely to be undone. Whether it will prove an act of wisdom or of shortsightedness only the future can tell.

The transition from the Italian Trentino to the German Tyrol begins a few miles south of Bozen. Perhaps "occurs" would be a more descriptive word, for the change from the Latin to the Teutonic, instead of being gradual, as one would expect, is almost startling in its abruptness. In the space of a single mile or so the language of the inhabitants changes from the liquid accents of the Latin to the deep-throated gutturals of the German; the road signs and those on the shops are now printed in quaint German script; *via* becomes *weg*, *strada* becomes *strasse*, instead of responding to your salutation with a smiling *"Bon giorno"* the peasants give you a solemn *"Guten morgen.*" Even the architecture changes, the slender, four-square campaniles surmounted by bulging Byzantine domes, so characteristic of the Trentino, giving place to pointed steeples faced with colored slates or tiles. On the German side the towns are better kept, the houses better built, the streets wider and cleaner than in the Italian districts. Instead of the low, white-walled, red-tiled dwellings so characteristic of Italy, the houses begin to assume the aspect of Alpine chalets, with carved wooden balconies and steep-pitched roofs to prevent the settling of the winter snows. The plastered façades of many of the houses are decorated with gaudily colored frescoes, nearly always of Biblical characters or scenes, so that in a score of miles the traveler has had the whole story of the Scriptures spread before him. They are a deeply religious people, these Tyrolean peasants, as is evidenced not only by the many handsome churches and the character of the wall-paintings on the houses, but by the amazing frequency of the wayside shrines, most of which consist of representations of various phases of the Crucifixion, usually carved and painted with a most harrowing fidelity of detail. Occasionally we encountered groups of peasants wearing the picturesque velvet jackets, tight knee-breeches, heavy woolen stockings and beribboned hats which one usually associates with the Tyrolean yodelers who still inflict themselves on vaudeville audiences in the United States. As we sped northward the landscape changed with the inhabitants, the sunny Italian countryside, ablaze with flowers and green with vineyards, giving way to solemn forests, gloomy defiles, and crags surmounted by grim, gray castles which reminded me of the stage-settings for "Tannhäuser" and "Lohengrin."

Seen from the summit of the Mendel Pass, the road from Trent to Bozen looks like a lariat thrown carelessly upon the ground. It climbs laboriously upward, through splendid evergreen forests, in countless curves and spirals, loiters for a few-score yards beside the margin of a tiny crystal lake, and then, refreshed, plunges downward, in a series of steep white zigzags, to meet the Isarco, in whose company it enters Bozen. Because the car, like ourselves, was thirsty, we stopped at the summit of the pass at the tiny hamlet of Madonna di

Campiglio—Our Lady of the Fields—for water and for tea. Should you have occasion to go that way, I hope that you will take time to stop at the unpretentious little Hotel Neumann. It is the sort of Tyrolean inn which had, I supposed, gone out of existence with the war. The innkeeper, a jovial, white-whiskered fellow, such as one rarely finds off the musical comedy stage, served us with tea—with rum in it—and hot bread with honey, and heaping dishes of small wild strawberries, and those pastries which the Viennese used to make in such perfection. There were five of us, including the chauffeur and the orderly, and for the food which we consumed I think that the innkeeper charged the equivalent of a dollar. But, as he explained apologetically, the war had raised prices terribly. We were the first visitors, it seemed, barring Austrians and a few Italian officers, who had visited his inn in nearly five years. Both of his sons had been killed in the war, he told us, fighting bravely with their Jaeger battalion. The widow of one of his sons—I saw her; a sweet-faced Austrian girl—with her child, had come to live with him, he said. Yes, he was an old man, both of his boys were dead, his little business had been wrecked, the old Emperor Franz-Joseph—yes, we could see his picture over the fireplace within—had gone and the new Emperor Karl was in exile, in Switzerland, life had heard; even the Empire in which he had lived, boy and man, for seventy-odd years, had disappeared; the whole world was, indeed, turned upside down—but, Heaven be praised, he had a little grandson who would grow up to carry the business on.

"How do you feel," I asked the old man, "about Italian rule?"

"They are not our own people," he answered slowly. "Their language is not our language and their ways are not our ways. But they are not an unkind nor an unjust people and I think that they mean to treat us fairly and well. Austria is very poor, I hear, and could do nothing for us if she would. But Italy is young and strong and rich and the officers who have stopped here tell me that she is prepared to do much to help us. Who knows? Perhaps it is all for the best."

The New Frontiers of Freedom: From the Alps to the Aegean

A LITTLE MOTHER OF THE TYROL
We gave her some candy: it was the first taste of sugar that she had had in four years

Immediately beyond Madonna di Campiglio the highway begins its descent from the pass in a series of appallingly sharp turns. Hardly had we settled ourselves in the tonneau before the Sicilian, impatient to be gone, stepped on the accelerator and the big Lancia, flinging itself over the brow of the hill, plunged headlong for the first of these hairpin turns. "Slow up!" I shouted. "Slow up or you'll have us over the edge!" As the driver's only response to my command was to grin at us reassuringly over his shoulder, I looked about for a soft place to land. But there was only rock-plated highway whizzing past and on the outside the road dropped sheer away into nothingness. We took the first turn with the near-side wheels in the gutter, the off-side wheels on the bank, and the car tilted at an angle of forty-five degrees. The second bend we navigated at an angle of sixty degrees, the off-side wheels on the bank, the near-side wheels pawing thin air. Had there been another bend immediately following we should have accomplished it upside down. Fortunately there were no more for the moment, but there remained the village street of Cles. We pounced upon it like a tiger on its prey. Shrilling, roaring and honking, we swooped through the ancient town, zigzagging from curb to curb. The great-great-grandam of the village was tottering across the street when the blast of the Lancia's siren pierced the deafness of a century and she sprang for the sidewalk with the agility of a young gazelle. We missed her by half an inch, but at the next corner we had better luck and killed a chicken.

Meran—the Italians have changed its official name to Merano, just as they have changed Trent to Trento, and Bozen to Bolzano—has always appealed to me as one of the most charming and restful little towns in Europe. The last time I had been there, before the war-cloud darkened the land, its streets were lined with powerful touring cars bearing the license-plates of half the countries in Europe, bands played in the parks, the shady promenade beside the river was crowded with pleasure-seekers, and its great tourist hostelries—there were said to be upwards of 150 hotels and *pensions* in the town—were gay with laughter and music. But this time all was changed. Most of the large hotels were closed, the streets were deserted, the place was as dismal as a cemetery. It reminded me of a beautiful house which has been closed because of its owner's financial reverses, the servants discharged, the windows boarded up, the furniture swathed in linen covers, the carpets and hangings packed away in mothballs, and the gardens overrun with weeds. At the Hotel Savoy, where rooms had been reserved for us, it was necessary, in pre-war days, to wire for accommodations a fortnight in advance of your arrival, and even then you were not always able to get rooms. Yet we were the only visitors, barring a handful of

Italian commercial travelers and the Italian governor-general and his staff. The proprietor, an Austrian, told me that in the four years of war he had lost $300,000, and that he, like his colleagues, was running his hotel on borrowed money. Of the pre-war visitors to Meran, eighty per cent. had been Germans, he told me, adding that he could see no prospect of the town's regaining its former prosperity until Germany is on her financial feet again. Personally, I think that he and the other hoteliers and business men with whom I talked in Meran were rather more pessimistic than the situation warranted, for, if Italy will have the foresight to do for these new playgrounds of hers in the Alps even a fraction of what she has done for her resorts on the Riviera, and in Sicily, and along the Neapolitan littoral, if she will advertise and encourage and assist them, if she will maintain their superb roads and improve their railway communications, then I believe that a few years, a very few, will see them thronged by even greater crowds of visitors than before the war. And the fact that in the future there will be more American, English, French and Italian visitors, and fewer Germans, will make South Tyrol a far pleasanter place to travel in.

The Italians are fully alive to the gravity of the problems which confront them in attempting to assimilate a body of people, as courageous, as sturdily independent, and as tenacious of their traditional independence as these Tyrolean mountaineers—descendants of those peasants, remember, who, led by Andreas Hofer, successfully defied the dictates of Napoleon. Though I think that she is going about the business of assimilating these unwilling subjects with tact and common sense, I do not envy Italy her task. Generally speaking, the sympathy of the world is always with a weak people as opposed to a strong one, as England discovered when she attempted to impose her rule upon the Boers. Once let the Italian administration of the Upper Adige permit itself to be provoked into undue harshness (and there will be ample provocation; be certain of that); once let an impatient and over-zealous governor-general attempt to bend these stubborn mountaineers too abruptly to his will; let the local Italian officials provide the slightest excuse for charges of injustice or oppression, and Italy will have on her hands in Tyrol far graver troubles than those brought on by her adventure in Tripolitania.

The New Frontiers of Freedom: From the Alps to the Aegean

Though the Government has announced that Italian must become the official language of the newly acquired region, and that used in its schools, no attempt will be made to root out the German tongue or to tamper with the local usages and customs. The upper valleys, where German is spoken, will not, however, enjoy any form of local autonomy which would tend to set their inhabitants apart from those of the lower valleys, for it is realized that such differential treatment would only serve to retard the process of unification. All of the new districts, German and Italian-speaking alike, will be included in the new province of Trent. It is entirely probable that Italy's German-speaking subjects of the present generation will prove, if not actually irreconcilable, at least mistrustful and resentful, but, by adhering to a policy of patience, sympathy, generosity and tact, I can see no reason why the next generation of these mountaineers should not prove as loyal Italians as though their fathers had been born under the cross of the House of Savoy instead of under the double-eagle of the Hapsburgs.

We crossed the Line of the Armistice into Austria an hour or so beyond Meran, the road being barred at this point by a swinging beam, made from the trunk of a tree, which could be swung aside to permit the passage of vehicles, like the bar of an old-fashioned country toll-gate. Close by was a rude shelter, built of logs, which provided sleeping quarters for the half-company of infantry engaged in guarding the pass. One has only to cross the new frontier to understand why Italy was so desperately insistent on a strategic rectification of her northern boundary, for whereas, before the war, the frontier ran through the valleys, leaving the Austrians atop the mountain wall, it is now the Italians who are astride the wall, with the Austrians in the valleys below.

No sooner had we crossed the Line of the Armistice than we noticed an abrupt change in the attitude of the population. Even in the German-speaking districts of the Trentino the inhabitants with whom we had come in contact had been courteous and respectful, though whether this was because of, or in spite of, the fact that we were traveling in a military car, accompanied by a staff-officer, I do not know. Now that we were actually in Austria, however, this atmosphere of seeming friendliness entirely disappeared, the men staring insolently at us from under scowling brows, while the women and children, who had less to fear and consequently were bolder in expressing their feelings, frequently shouted uncomplimentary epithets at us or shook their fists as we passed.

ITALY'S NEW FRONTIER
A sharp turn on the highroad over the Brenner Pass

Under the terms of the Armistice, Innsbruck, the capital of Tyrol, was temporarily occupied by the Italians, who sent into the city a comparatively small force, consisting in the main of Alpini and Bersaglieri. Innsbruck was one of the proudest cities of the Austrian Empire, its inhabitants being noted for their loyalty to the Hapsburgs, yet I did not observe the slightest sign of resentment toward the Italian soldiers, who strolled the streets and made purchases in the shops as unconcernedly as though they were in Milan or Rome. The Italians, on their part, showed the most marked consideration for the sensibilities of the population, displaying none of the hatred and contempt for their former enemies which characterized the French armies of occupation on the Rhine.

We found that rooms had been reserved for us at the Tyroler Hof, before the war one of the famous tourist hostelries of Europe, half of which had been taken over by the Italian general commanding in the Innsbruck district and his staff. Food was desperately scarce in Innsbruck when we were there and, had it not been for the courtesy of the Italian commander in sending us in dishes from his mess, we would have had great difficulty in getting enough to eat. A typical dinner at the Tyroler Hof in the summer of 1919 consisted of a mud-colored, nauseous-looking liquid which was by courtesy called soup, a piece of fish perhaps four times the size of a postage-stamp, a stew which was alleged to consist of rabbit and vegetables but which, from its taste and appearance, might contain almost anything, a salad made of beets or watercress, but without oil, and for dessert a dish of wild berries, which are abundant in parts of Tyrol. There was an extra charge for a small cup of black coffee, so-called, which was made, I imagine, from acorns. This, of course, was at the best and highest-priced hotels in Innsbruck; at the smaller hotels the food was correspondingly scarcer and poorer.

Though the inhabitants of the rural districts appeared to be moderately well fed, a majority of the people of Innsbruck were manifestly in urgent need of food. Some of them, indeed, were in a truly pitiable condition, with emaciated bodies, sunken cheeks, unhealthy complexions, and shabby, badly worn clothes. The meager displays in the shop-windows were a pathetic contrast to variety and abundance which characterized them in ante-bellum days, the only articles displayed in any profusion being picture-postcards, objects carved from wood and similar souvenirs. The windows of the confectionery and bake-shops were particularly noticeable for the paucity of their contents. I was induced to enter one of them by a brave window display of hand-decorated candy boxes, but, upon investigation, it proved that the boxes were empty and that the shop had had no candy for four years. The prices of necessities, such as food and clothing, were fantastic (I saw advertisements of stout, all-leather boots for rent to responsible persons by the day or week), but articles of a purely luxurious character could be had for almost anything one was willing to offer. In one shop I was shown German field-glasses of high magnification and the finest makes for ten and fifteen dollars a pair. The local jewelers were driving a brisk trade with the Italian soldiers, who were lavish purchasers of Austrian war medals and decorations. Captain Tron bought an Iron Cross of the second class for the equivalent of thirty cents.

We left Innsbruck in the early morning with the intention of spending that night at Cortina d'Ampezzo, but, owing to our unfamiliarity with the roads and to delays due to tire trouble, nightfall found us lost in the Dolomites. For mile after mile we pushed on through the darkness along the narrow, slippery mountain roads, searching for a shelter in which to pass the night. Occasionally the twin beams from our lamps would illumine a building beside the road and we, chilled and hungry, would exclaim "A house at last!" only to find, upon drawing nearer, that, though it had evidently been once a habitation, it was now but a shattered, blackened shell, a grim testimonial to the accuracy of Austrian and Italian gunners. It was late in the evening and bitterly cold, before, rounding a shoulder of the mountain up whose steep gradients the car seemed to have been panting for ages, we saw in the distance the welcome lights of the hamlet of Santa Lucia.

I do not think that the public has the slightest conception of the widespread destruction and misery wrought by the war in these Alpine regions. In nearly a hundred miles of motoring in the Cadore, formerly one of the most delightful summer playgrounds in all Europe, we did not pass a single building with a whole roof or an unshattered wall. The hospitable wayside inns, the quaint villages, the picturesque peasant cottages which the tourist in this region knew and loved are but blackened ruins now. And the people are gone too—refugees, no doubt, in the camps which the Government has erected for them near the larger towns. One no longer hears the tinkle of cow-bells on the mountain slopes, peasants no longer wave a friendly greeting from their doors: it is a stricken and deserted land. But Cortina d'Ampezzo, which is the *cheflieu* of the Cadore, though still showing many traces of the shell-storms which it has survived, was quickening into life. The big tourist hotels at either end of the town, behind which the Italians emplaced their heavy guns, were being refurnished in anticipation of the resumption of summer travel and the little shops where they sell souvenirs were reopening, one by one. But the losses suffered by the inhabitants of these Alpine valleys, desperately serious as they are to them, are, after all, but insignificant when compared with the enormous havoc wrought by the armies in the thickly settled Friuli and on the rich Venetian plains. Every one knows, presumably, that Italy had to draw more heavily upon her resources than any other country among the Allies *(did you know that she spent in the war more than four-fifths of her total national wealth?)* and that she is bowed down under an enormous load of taxation and a staggering burden of debt. But what has been largely overlooked is that she is faced by the necessity of rebuilding a vast devastated area, in which the conditions are quite as serious, the need of assistance fully as urgent, as in the devastated regions of Belgium and France.

Probably you were not aware that a territory of some three and a half million acres, occupied by nearly a million and a half people, was overrun by the Austrians. More than one-half of Venetia is comprised in that region lying east of the Piave where the wave of Hunnish invasion broke with its greatest fury. The whole of Udine and Belluno, and parts of Treviso, Vicenza and Venice suffered the penalty of standing in the path of the Hun. They were prosperous provinces, agriculturally and industrially, but now both industry and agriculture are almost at a standstill, for their factories have been burned, their machinery wrecked or stolen, their livestock driven off and their vineyards destroyed. The damage done is estimated at 500 million dollars. It is unnecessary for me to emphasize the seriousness of the problem which thus confronts the Italian Government. Not only must it provide food and shelter for the homeless—a problem which it has solved by the erection of great numbers of wooden huts somewhat similar to the barracks at the American cantonments—but a great amount of livestock and machinery must be supplied before industry can be resumed. At one period there was such desperate need of fuel that even the olive trees, one of the region's chief sources of revenue, were sacrificed. The Italians have set about the task of regeneration with an energy that discouragement cannot check. But the undertaking is more than Italy can accomplish unaided, for the resources of her other provinces are seriously depleted. We are fond of talking of the debt we owe to Italy, not merely for her sacrifices in the war, but for all that she has given us in art and music and literature. Now is the time to show our gratitude.

From Cortina, which is Italian now, we swung toward the north again, re-crossed the Line of the Armistice at Tarvis, and, just as night was falling, came tearing into Villach, which, like Innsbruck, was occupied, under the terms of the Armistice, by Italian troops. We had great difficulty in obtaining rooms in Villach, not because there were no rooms but because we were accompanied by an Italian officer and were traveling in an Italian car. The proprietors of five hotels, upon seeing Captain Tron's uniform, curtly declared that every room was occupied. It was nearly midnight before we succeeded in finding shelter for the night, and this was obtained only when I made it amply clear to the Austrian proprietor of the only remaining hotel in the town that we were not Italians but Americans. The unpleasant impression produced by the coolness of our reception in Villach was materially increased the following morning, when Captain Tron greeted us with the news that all of our luggage, which we had left on the car, had been stolen. It seemed that thieves had broken into the courtyard of the barracks, where the car had been locked up for the night, and, in spite of the fact that the chauffeur was asleep in the tonneau, had stripped it of everything, including the spare tires. I learned afterwards that robberies of this sort had become so common since the war as scarcely to provoke comment, portions of Austria being terrorized by gangs of demobilized soldiers who, taking advantage of the complete demoralization of the machinery of government, robbed farmhouses and plundered travelers at will. It is much the same form of lawlessness, I imagine, which manifested itself immediately after the close of the Napoleonic Wars, when bands of discharged soldiers sought in robbery the excitement and booty which they had formerly found under the eagles. Though the local police authorities attempted to condone the robbery on the ground that it was due to the appalling poverty of the population, this excuse did not reconcile my wife to the loss of her entire wardrobe. As she remarked vindictively, she felt certain that the inhabitants of Villach were called Villains.

I wished to visit Klagenfurt, the ancient capital of Carinthia, which is about twenty miles beyond Villach, because at that time the town, which is a railway junction of considerable strategic and commercial importance, threatened to provide the cause for an open break between the Jugoslavs and the Italians. Though the Italians did not demand the town for themselves, they had vigorously insisted that, instead of being awarded to Jugoslavia, it should remain Austrian, for, with the triangle of which Klagenfurt is the center in the possession of the Jugoslavs, they would have driven a wedge between Italy and Austria and would have had under their control the immensely important junction-point where the main trunk line from Venice to Vienna is joined by the line coming up from Fiume and Trieste. The Jugoslavs, recognizing that the possession of Klagenfurt would give them virtual control of the principal railway entering Austria from the south, and that such control would probably enable them to divert much of Austria's traffic from the Italian ports of Venice and Trieste to their own port of Fiume, which they confidently expected would be awarded them by the Peace Conference, lost no time in occupying the town with a considerable force of troops. They further justified this occupation by asserting that Jugoslavia was entitled to Carinthia on ethnological grounds and that the inhabitants of Klagenfurt were clamoring for Jugoslav rule. In view of these developments, I had expected to find Jugoslav soldiery in the town, but I had not expected to be challenged, a mile or so outside the town, by a sentry who was, judging from his appearance, straight from a *comitadji* band in the Macedonian mountains. He was a sullen-faced fellow wearing a fur cap and a nondescript uniform, with an assortment of weapons thrust in his belt, according to the custom of the Balkan guerrillas, and with two bandoliers, stuffed with cartridges, slung across his chest. He was as incongruous a figure in that pleasant German countryside as one of Pancho Villa's bandits would have been in the Connecticut Valley. And Klagenfurt, which is a well-built, well-paved, thoroughly modern Austrian town, was occupied by several hundred of his fellows, brought from somewhere in the Balkans, I should imagine, for the express purpose of aweing the population. It was perfectly apparent that the inhabitants, far from welcoming these fierce-looking fighters as brother-Slavs and friends, were only too anxious to have them take their departure, having about as much in common with them, in appearance, manners and speech, as a New Englander has with an Apache Indian. So great was the tension existing in Klagenfurt that a commission had been sent by the Peace Conference to study the question on the spot, its members communicating with the Supreme Council in Paris by means of American couriers, slim young fellows in khaki who wore on their arms the blue brassard, embroidered with the scales of justice, which was the badge of messengers employed by the Peace Commission.

A few miles outside of Klagenfurt my attention was attracted by an iron paling, in a field beside the road, enclosing a gigantic chair carved from stone. My curiosity aroused, I stopped the car to examine it. From a faded inscription attached to the gate I learned that this was the crowning chair of the Dukes of Carinthia, in which the ancient rulers of this region had sat to be crowned. There it stands in a field beside the highway, neglected and forgotten, a curious link with a picturesque and far-distant past.

Our route from Klagenfurt led back through Villach to Tarvis and thence over the Predil Pass to the Friuli plain and Udine, a journey which we expected to accomplish in a single day; but there were delays in re-crossing the Line of the Armistice and other and more serious delays in the mountains, caused by torrential rains which had in places washed out the road, so that it was already nightfall when, emerging from the gloomy defile of the Predil Pass, we saw before us the twinkling lights of the Alpini cantonment at Caporetto, that mountain hamlet of black memories where, in the summer of 1917, the Austro-German armies, aided by bad Italian generalship and Italian treachery, smashed through the Italian lines and forced them back in a headlong retreat which was checked only by the heroic stand on the Piave. The Caporetto disaster would have broken the hearts and annihilated the resistance of a less courageous people than the Italians. Yet the Italian army, shattered and disorganized as it was, stopped the triumphant progress of the invaders; stopped it almost without artillery or ammunition, for hundreds of guns had been abandoned during the retreat; stopped it with the bodies of Italy's youth, the boys fresh from the training-camps, the class of 1919, called to the colors two years before their time! They stopped that victorious rush upon the line of the Piave, a broad, shallow stream meandering through a flat plain with never a height to command the enemy's positions, never a physical feature of the terrain to satisfy the requirements of strategy. Not only was the line of the Piave held by the Italians against the advice of their Allies, but it was held in defiance of all the lessons taught by Italian history, for that the Piave could not be successfully defended has been the judgment of every military leader since first the barbarians began to sweep down from the Alps to lay waste the rich Venetian plain. The Italians made their heroic stand, moreover, without any help from their Allies. That help came later, it is true, but only after the stand had been made. You doubt this? Then read this extract from the report of General the Earl of Caven, who commanded the Allied troops sent to the aid of the Italians:

"In 1917, in the terrible days which followed the disaster at Caporetto, I saw, just after my arrival at Venice, the Italian army in full retreat, and I became convinced that a recovery was impossible before the arrival of sufficient reenforcement from France and England. But I was deceived, for shortly afterward I saw the Italian army, which had seemed to be in the advanced stages of an utter rout, form a solid line on the Piave and hold it with miraculous persistence, permitting the English and French reenforcements to take up the positions assigned to them without once coming in contact with the enemy."

I have heard it said by critics of Italy that the retreat from Caporetto showed the lack of courage of the Italian soldier. To gauge the courage of an army a single disaster is as unjust as it is unintelligent.

Was the rout of the Federal forces at Bull Run a criterion of their behavior in the succeeding years of the Civil War? Was the surrender at Sedan a true indication of the fighting ability of the French soldier? Every nation has had its disasters and has had to live them down. Italy did this when, on the banks of Piave, she turned her greatest disaster into her most glorious triumph.

Because it was my privilege to be with the Italian army in the field during various periods of the war, and because I know at first-hand whereof I speak, I regret and resent the disparagement of the Italian soldier which has been so freely indulged in since the Armistice. It may be, of course, that you do not fully realize the magnitude of Italy's sacrifices and achievements. Did you know, for example, that Italy held a front longer than the British, Belgian, French and American fronts put together? Did you know that out of a population of 37 millions she put into the field an army of 5 million men, whereas France and her colonies, with nearly double the population, was never able to raise more than 5,064,000, a considerable proportion of which were black and brown men? Did you know that in forty-one months of war Italy lost 541,000 in dead and 953,000 in wounded, and that, unlike France and England, her armies were composed wholly of white men? Did you know that, in spite of all that has been said about the Allies giving her assistance, Italy at all times had more troops on the Western front than the Allies had on the Italian? Did you know that she called up the class of 1919 two years before their time, a measure which even France, hard-pressed as she was, did not feel justified in taking? (I have mentioned this before, but it will bear repetition.) Have you stopped to think that she was the only one of the Allied nations which won a clean-cut and decisive victory, when, on the Piave, she attacked with 51 divisions an Austro-German army of 63 divisions, completely smashed it, forced its surrender, and captured half a million prisoners? Did you know that she lost more than fifty-seven per cent, of her merchant tonnage, while England lost less than forty-three per cent, and France less than forty per cent.? And, finally, had you realized that Italy made greater sacrifices, in proportion to her resources and population, than any other country engaged in the war, having devoted four-fifths of her entire national wealth to the prosecution of the struggle? There is your answer, chapter and verse, for the next man who sneeringly remarks, "The Italians didn't do much, did they?"

Just as the Trentino and the Upper Adige have been added to the kingdom as the Province of Trent, so the redeemed regions of which Trieste is the center, including the towns of Gorizia, Monfalcone, Capodistria, Parenzo, Pirano, Rovigno and Pola, have been consolidated in the new province of Julian Venetia, with about a million inhabitants and an area of approximately 6,000 square miles.

THIS IS NOT VENICE, AS YOU MIGHT SUPPOSE, BUT TRIESTE
The sails of the fishing craft are of many colors, yellow, burnt-orange, vermilion. At the head of the canal, its stately columns reflected in the turquoise waters, the Bourse rises like some ancient Roman temple

Trieste, which, with its suburbs, has a population of not far from 400,000, with its splendid terminal facilities, its vast harbor-works, its dry-docks and foundries, its railway communications with the hinterland, and, above all else, its position as the natural outlet for the trade of Austria, Bavaria and Czecho-Slovakia, constitutes not only Italy's most valuable prize of war, but, everything considered, probably the most important city, commercially at least, to change hands as a result of the conflict. Curiously enough, Trieste is the least interesting city of its size, from a visitor's point of view, that I know.

The New Frontiers of Freedom: From the Alps to the Aegean

Venice always reminds me of a beautiful and charmingly gowned woman, perpetually young, interested in art, in music, in literature, always ready for a stroll, a dance or a flirtation. Trieste, on the contrary, is a busy, preoccupied, rather brusque business man, wholly self-made, who has never devoted much time to devote to pleasure because he has been too busy making his fortune. Venice says, "If you want a good time, let me show you how to spend your money." But Trieste growls, "If you want to get rich, let me show you how to invest your money." The city has broad and well-kept streets bordered by the same sort of four-and five-and six-story buildings of brick and stone which you find in any European commercial city; it has several unusually spacious piazzas on which front some really pretentious buildings; it has a few arches and doorways dating from the Roman period, though far better ones can be found in almost any town on the Italian peninsula; on the hill commanding the city there are an old Austrian fort and an ancient church, both chiefly interesting for the views they command of the harbor and the coast of Istria; some of the most abominably rough pavements which I have ever encountered in any city; one hotel which just escapes being excellent and several which do not escape being bad; and a harbor, together with the wharves and moles and machinery which go with it, which is the Triestino's pride and joy.

To my way of thinking the most interesting sight in Trieste is a small château, built in the castellated fashion which had a considerable vogue in America shortly after the close of the Civil War, which stands amid most beautiful gardens on the edge of the sea, two or three miles to the west of the city. This is the Château of Miramar, formerly the residence of the young Austrian Archduke Maximilian, who, dazzled by the dream of life on an imperial throne, accepted an invitation to become Emperor of Mexico and a few years later fell before a Mexican firing-party on the slopes of Queretaro. Though the château has now passed into the possession of the Italian Government it is still in charge of the aged custodian who, as a youth, was body-servant to Maximilian. Barring the fact that the paintings and certain pieces of furniture had been removed to Vienna to save from injury by aerial bombardment, the interior of the château is much as Maximilian left it when he set out with his bride, Carlotta, the sister of the late King Leopold of the Belgians, on his ill-fated adventure. In the study on the ground floor hangs a photograph, still sharp and clear after the lapse of half a century, of the members of the delegation—swarthy men in the high cravats and long frock-coats of the period, some of them wearing the stars and sashes of orders—who came to Miramar to offer Maximilian the Mexican crown. The old custodian told me that he witnessed the scene and he pointed out to me where his young master and the other actors in this, the first act of the tragedy, stood. How little could the youthful Emperor have dreamed, as he set sail for those distant shores, that the day would come when the Dual Monarchy would go down in ruins, when the ancient dynasty of the Hapsburgs would come to an inglorious end, and when the garden paths where he and his beautiful young bride used to saunter in the moonlight would be paced by Italian carabineers.

If you will get out the atlas and turn to the map of Italy you will notice at the head of the Adriatic a peninsula shaped like the head of an Indian arrow, its tip aimed toward the unprotected flank of Italy's eastern coast. This arrow-shaped peninsula is Istria. In the western notch of the arrowhead, toward Italy, is Trieste—terminus of the railway to Vienna. In the opposite notch is Fiume—terminus of the railway which runs across Croatia and Hungary to Budapest. And at the very tip of the arrow, as though it had been ground to a deadly sharpness, is Pola, formerly Austria's greatest naval base. Dotting the western coast of Istria, between Trieste and Pola, are four small towns—Parenzo, Pirano, Capodistria and Rovigno—all purely and distinctively Italian, and, on the other side of the peninsula, the famous resort of Abbazia, popular with wealthy Hungarians and with the yachtsmen of all nations before the war.

Parenzo, Pirano, Capodistria and Rovigno were all outposts of the Venetian Republic, forming an outer line of defense against the Slav barbarians of the interior. Everything about them speaks of Venice: the snarling Lion of St. Mark which is carved above their gates and surmounts the marble columns in their piazzas; their old, old churches—the one at Parenzo was built in the sixth century, being copied after the famous basilica at Ravenna, across the Adriatic—the interiors of many of them adorned, like that of St. Mark's in Venice, with superb mosaics of gold and semi-precious stones; the carved lions' heads, *bocca del leone*, for receiving secret missives; the delicate tracery above the doors and windows of the palazzos, and all those other architectural features so characteristic of the City of the Doges. There is no questioning what these Istrian coast-towns were or are. They are as Italian to-day as when, a thousand years ago, they formed a part of Venice's far-flung skirmish line. But penetrate even a single mile into the interior of the peninsula and you find a wholly different race from these Latins of the littoral, a different architecture (if architecture can be applied to square huts built of sun-dried bricks) and a different tongue. These people are the Croats, a hardy, industrious agricultural people, generally illiterate, at least as I found them in Istria, and with few of the comforts and none of the culture which characterized the Latin communities on the coast. In short, the towns of the western coast are undeniably Italian; the rest of the peninsula is solidly Slav.

The interior of Istria consists, in the main, of a barren, monotonous and peculiarly unlovely limestone plateau known as the Karst, a continuation of that waterless and treeless ridge, called by Italians the Carso, which stretches from Trieste northwestward to Goritzia and beyond. With the exception of the Bukovica of Dalmatia and the lava-beds of southern Utah, the Istrian Karst is the most utterly hopeless region, from the standpoint of agriculture, that I know. It is dotted with many small farmsteads, it is true, but one marvels at the courage and patience which their peasant owners displayed in their unequal struggle with Nature. The rocky surface is covered with a stunted, discouraged-looking vegetation which reminded me of that clothing the flanks of the mountains in the vicinity of the Roosevelt Dam, in Arizona, and here and there are vast rolling moors, uninhabited by man or animal, as desolate, mysterious and repelling as that depicted by Sir Arthur Conan Doyle in *The Hound of the Baskervilles*. The Karst, like the Carso, is dotted with curious depressions called *dolinas*, some of them as much as 100 feet in depth, the floors of which, varying in extent from a few square yards to several acres, are covered with soil which is as rich as the surface of the surrounding plateau is worthless. Because of the fertility of these singular depressions, and their immunity from the cold winds which in winter sweep the surface of the Karst, they are utilized by the peasants for growing fruits, vegetables and, in some cases, small patches of grain, being, in effect, sunken gardens provided by Nature as though to recompense the Istrians, in some measure, for their discouraging struggle for existence.

Just behind the very tip of the peninsula, on the edge of a superb natural harbor, the entrance to which is masked by the Brioni Islands, is the great naval base of Pola, from the shelter of whose fortifications and mined approaches the Austrian fleet was able to terrorize the defenseless towns along Italy's unprotected eastern seaboard and to menace the commerce of the northern Adriatic. Pola Is a strange mélange of the ancient and the modern, for from the topmost tiers of the great Roman Arena—scarcely less imposing than the Coliseum at Rome—we looked down upon a harbor dotted with the fighting monsters of the Italian navy, while all day long Italian seaplanes swooped and circled over the splendid arch, erected by a Roman emperor in the dim dawn of European history, to commemorate his triumph over the barbarians.

It is just such anomalies as these that make almost impossible the solution, on a basis of strict justice to the inhabitants, of the Adriatic problem. Here you see a city that, in history, in population, in language, is as characteristically Italian as though it were under the shadow of the Apennines, yet encircling that city is a countryside whose inhabitants are wholly Slav, who are intensely hostile to Italian institutions, and many of whom have no knowledge whatsoever of the Italian tongue. The Italians claim that Istria should be theirs because of the undoubted Latin character of the towns along its coasts, because their Roman and Venetian ancestors established their outposts here long centuries ago, because the only culture that the region possesses is Italian, and, above all else, because its possession is essential to the safety of Italy herself. The Slavs, on the other hand, lay claim to Istria on the ground that its first inhabitants, whether barbarians or not, were Slavs, that the Italians who settled on its shores were but filibusters and adventurers, and that its inhabitants, by blood, by language, and by sentiment, are overwhelmingly Slav to-day. The only thing on which both races agree is that the peninsula should not be divided. It was no easy problem, you see, which the peace-makers were expected to solve with strict justice for all. If my memory serves me right, King

Solomon was once called upon by two mothers to settle a somewhat similar dispute, though in that case it was a child instead of a country whose ownership was in question. So, though both Latins and Slavs may continue to assert their rights to the peninsula in its entirety, I imagine that the Istrian problem will eventually be settled by the judgment of Solomon.

CHAPTER II

THE BORDERLAND OF SLAV AND LATIN

It was the same along the entire line of the Armistice from the Brenner down to Istria. Whenever the officials with whom we talked heard that we were going to Fiume, they shook their heads pessimistically. "It's a good place to stay away from just now," said one. "They won't let you enter the city," another warned us. Or, "You mustn't think of taking the *signora* with you." But the representative of an American oil company whom I met in the American consulate in Trieste regarded the excursion from a different view-point altogether.

"Be sure to stop at the Europa," he urged me. "It's right on the water-front, and there isn't a better place in the city to see what's happening. I was there last week when the mob attacked the French Annamite troops. Believe me, friend, that was one hellish business ... they literally cut those poor little Chinks into pieces. I saw the whole thing from my window. I'm going back to Fiume to-morrow, and if you like I'll tell the manager of the Europa to save you a front room."

His tone was that of a New Yorker telling a friend from up-State that he would reserve him a room in a Fifth Avenue hotel from which to view a parade.

As things turned out, however, we did not have occasion to avail ourselves of this offer, for we found that rooms had been reserved for us at a hotel in Abbazia, just across the bay from Fiume. This arrangement was due to the Italian military governor, General Grazioli, who was perfectly aware that the inhabitants of Fiume were not hanging out any "Welcome-to-Our-City" signs for foreigners, particularly for foreigners who were country people of President Wilson, and that the fewer Americans there were in the town the less danger there was of anti-American demonstrations. In view of what had happened to the Annamites I had no overpowering desire to be the center of a similar demonstration. Pursuant to this arrangement we slept in a great barn of a hotel whose echoing corridors had, in happier days, been a favorite resort of the wealth and fashion of Hungary, but whose once costly furniture had been sadly dilapidated by the spurred boots of the Austrian staff officers who had used it as a headquarters; in the mornings we had our sugarless coffee and butterless war-bread on a lofty balcony commanding a superb panorama of the Istrian coast from Icici to Volosca and of the island-studded Bay of Quarnero, and commuted to and from Fiume in the big gray Lancia in which we had traveled along the line of the Armistice for upward of 2,000 miles.

We had our first view of the Unredeemed City (though it was really not my first view, as I had been there before the war) from a curve in the road where it suddenly emerges from the woods of evergreen laurel above Volosca to drop in steep white zigzags to the sea. It is superbly situated, this ancient city over whose possession Slav and Latin are growling at each other like dogs over a disputed bone. With its snowy buildings spread on the slopes of a shallow amphitheater between the sapphire waters of the Adriatic and the barren flanks of the Istrian Karst, it suggested a lovely siren, all glistening and white, who had emerged from the sea to lie upon the bare brown breast of a mountain giant.

The car, with its exhaust wide open, for your Italian driver delights in noise, roared down the grade at express-train speed, took the hairpin curve at the bottom on two wheels, to be brought to an abrupt halt with an agonized squealing of brakes, our further progress being barred by a six-inch tree-trunk which had been lowered across the road like a barrier at an old-time country toll-gate. At one side of the road was a picket of Italian carabinieri in field-gray uniforms, their huge cocked hats rendered a shade less anachronistic by covers of gray linen, with carbines slung over their shoulders, hunter fashion. On the opposite side of the highway was a patrol of British sailors in white drill landing-kit, their rosy, smiling faces in striking contrast to the saturnine countenances of the Italians. (I might explain, parenthetically, that Fiume, being in theory under the jurisdiction of the Peace Conference, was at this time occupied by about a thousand French troops, the same number of British, a few score American blue-jackets, and nearly 10,000 Italians.) The sergeant in command of the carabinieri stepped up to the car, saluted, and curtly asked for our papers. I produced them. Among them was a pass authorizing us to go when and where we pleased in the territory occupied by the Italian forces. It had been given to me by the Minister of War himself, but it made about as much impression on the sergeant as though it had been signed by Charlie Chaplin.

"This is good only for Italy," he said. "It will not take you across the line of the Armistice."

AT THE GATES OF FIUME
Major Powell (second from left), Mrs. Powell, Captain Tron of the Italian Comando Supremo, and the car in which they travelled 1,000 miles

Thereupon I played my last trump. I produced an imposing document which had been given me by the Italian peace delegation in Paris. It had originally been issued by the Orlando-Sonnino cabinet, but upon the fall of that government I had had it countersigned, before leaving Rome, by the Nitti cabinet. It was addressed to all the military, naval, and civil authorities of Italy, and was so flatteringly worded that it would have satisfied St. Peter himself. But the sergeant was not in the least impressed. He read it through deliberately, scrutinized the official seals, examined the watermark, and then disappeared into a sentry-box on the roadside. I could hear him talking, evidently over a telephone. Presently he emerged and signaled to his men to raise the barrier. "Passo," he said grudgingly, in a tone which intimated that he was letting us enter the jealously guarded portals of Fiume against his better judgment, the bar swung upward, the big car leaped forward like a race-horse that feels the spur, and in another moment we were rolling through the tree-arched, stone-paved streets of the most-talked-of city in the world. As we sped down the Corsia Deák we passed a large hotel which, as was quite evident, had recently been renamed, for the words "Albergo d'Annunzio" were fresh and staring. But underneath was the former name, which had been so imperfectly obliterated that it could still easily be deciphered. It was "Hotel Wilson."

To correctly visualize Fiume you must imagine a town no larger than Atlantic City crowded upon a narrow shelf between a towering mountain wall and the sea; a town with broad and moderately clean streets, shaded, save in the center of the city, by double rows of stately trees and paved with large square flagstones which make abominably rough riding; a town with several fine thoroughfares bordered by well-constructed four-story buildings of brick and stone; with numerous surprisingly well-stocked shops; with miles and miles of concrete moles and wharfs, equipped with harbor machinery of the most modern description, and adjacent to them rows of warehouses as commodious as the Bush Terminals in Brooklyn, and rising here and there above the trees and the housetops, like fingers pointing to heaven, the graceful campaniles of fine old churches, one of which, the cathedral, was already old when the Great Navigator turned the prows of his caravels westward from Cadiz in quest of this land we live in.

Fiume lacks none of the conditions which make a great seaport: there is deep water and a convenient approach, which is protected against the ocean and against a hostile fleet by the islands of Veglia and Cherso and against the north winds by the rocky plateau of the Karst. Yet, despite its natural advantages and the millions which were spent in its development by the Hungarian Government, Fiume never developed into a port of the size and importance which the foreign commerce of Hungary would have seemed to require, this being largely due to its unfortunate geographical condition, for the dreary and inhospitable Karst completely shuts the city off from the interior, the numerous tunnels and steep gradients making rail transport by this route difficult and consequently expensive.

The public life of the city centers in the Piazza Adamich, a broad square on which front numerous hotels, restaurants, and coffeehouses, before which lounge, from midmorning until midnight, a considerable proportion of the Italian population, sipping *café nero*, or tall drinks concocted from sweet, bright-colored syrups, scanning the papers and discussing, with much noise and gesticulation, the political situation and the doings of the peace commissioners in Paris. Save only Barcelona, Fiume has the most excitable and irritable population of any city that I know. When we were there street disturbances were as frequent as dog-fights used to be in Constantinople before the Turks recognized that the best gloves are made from dogskins. As I have said, a few days before our arrival a mob had attacked and killed in most barbarous fashion a number of Annamite soldiers who were guarding a French warehouse on the quay. Several prominent Fumani with whom I talked attempted to justify the massacre on the ground that a French sailor had torn a ribbon bearing the motto *"Italia o Morte!"* from the breast of a woman of the town. They did not seem to regret the affair or to realize that it is just such occurrences which lead the Peace Conference to question the wisdom of subjecting the city's Slav minority to that sort of rule. As a result of the tense atmosphere which prevailed in the city, the nerves of the population were so on edge that when my car backfired with a series of violent explosions, the loungers in front of a near-by café jumped as though a bomb had been thrown among them. The patron saint of Fiume is, appropriately enough, St. Vitus.

In discussing the question of Fiume the mistake is almost invariably made of considering it as a single city, whereas it really consists of two distinct communities, Fiume and Sussak, bitterly antagonistic and differing in race, religion, language, politics, customs, and thought. A small river, the Rieka, no wider than the Erie Canal, divides the city into two parts, one Latin the other Slav, very much as the Rio Grande separates the American city of El Paso from the

Mexican town of Ciudad Juarez. On the left or west bank of the river is Fiume, with approximately 40,000 inhabitants, of whom very nearly three-fourths are Italian. Here are the wharfs, the harbor works, the rail-head, the municipal buildings, the hotels, and the business districts. But cross the Rieka by the single wooden bridge which connects Fiume with Sussak and you find yourself in a wholly different atmosphere. In a hundred paces you pass from a city which is three-quarters Italian to a town which is overwhelmingly Slav. There are about 4,500 people in Sussak, of whom only one-eighth are Italian. But let it be perfectly clear that Sussak is not Fiume. In proclaiming its annexation to Italy on the ground of self-determination, the National Council of Fiume did not include Sussak, which is a Croatian village in historically Croatian territory. It will be seen, therefore, that Sussak, which is not a part of Fiume but an entirely separate municipality, does not enter into the question at all. As for the territory immediately adjacent to Fiume on the north and east, it is as Slav as though it were in the heart of Serbia. To put it briefly, Fiume is an Italian island entirely surrounded by Slavs.

The violent self-assertiveness of the Fumani may be attributed to the large measure of autonomy which they have always enjoyed, Fiume's status as a free city having been definitely established by Ferdinand I in 1530, recognized by Maria Theresa in 1776 when she proclaimed it "a separate body annexed to the crown of Hungary," and by the Hungarian Government finally confirmed in 1868. Louis Kossuth admitted its extraterritorial character when he said that, even though the Magyar tongue should be enforced elsewhere as the medium of official communication, he considered that an exception "should be made in favor of a maritime city whose vocation was to welcome all nations led thither by commerce."

Though the Italian element of the population vociferously asserts its adherence to the slogan *"Italia o Morte!"* I am convinced that many of the more substantial and far-seeing citizens, if they dared freely to express their opinions, would be found to favor the restoration of the city's ancient autonomy under the ægis of the League of Nations. The Italians of Flume are at bottom, beneath their excitable and mercurial temperaments, a shrewd business people who have the commercial future of their city at heart. And they are intelligent enough to realize that, unless there be established some stable form of government which will propitiate the Slav minority as well as the Italian majority, the Slav nations of the hinterland will almost certainly divert their trade, on which Fiume's commercial importance entirely depends, to some non-Italian port, in which event the city would inevitably retrograde to the obscure fishing village which it was less than half a century ago.

In order that you may have before you a clear and comprehensive picture of this most perplexing and dangerous situation, which is so fraught with peril for the future peace of the world, suppose that I sketch for you, in the fewest word-strokes possible, the arguments of the rival claimants for fair Fiume's hand. Italy's claims may be classified under three heads: sentimental, commercial, and political. Her sentimental claims are based on the ground that the city's population, character, and history are overwhelmingly Italian. I have already stated that the Italians constitute about three-fourths of the total population of Fiume, the latest figures, as quoted in the United States Senate, giving 29,569 inhabitants to the Italians and 14,798 to the Slavs. There is no denying that the city has a distinctively Italian atmosphere, for its architecture is Italian, that Venetian trademark, the Lion of St. Mark, being in evidence on several of the older buildings; the mode of outdoor life is such as one meets in Italy; most of its stores and banks are owned by Italians, and Italian is the prevailing tongue. The claim that the city's history is Italian is, however, hardly borne out by history itself, for in the sixteen centuries which have elapsed since the fall of the Roman Empire, Fiume has been under Italian rule—that of the republic of Venice—for just four days.

The commercial reason underlying Italy's insistence on obtaining control of Fiume is due to the fact that Italians are convinced that should Fiume pass into either neutral or Jugoslav hands, it would mean the commercial ruin of Trieste, where enormous sums of Italian money have been invested. They assert, and with sound reasoning, that the Slavs of the hinterland, and probably the Germans and Magyars as well, would ship through Fiume, were it under Slav or international control, instead of through Trieste, which is Italian. One does not need to be an economist to realize that if Fiume could secure the trade of Jugoslavia and the other states carved from the Austro-Hungarian Empire, the commercial supremacy of Trieste, which depends upon this same hinterland, would quickly disappear. On the other hand, those Italians whose vision has not been distorted by their passions clearly foresee that, should the final disposition of Fiume prove unacceptable to the Jugoslavs, they will almost certainly divert the trade of the interior to some Slav port, leaving Fiume to drowse in idleness beside her moss-grown wharfs and crumbling warehouses, dreaming dreams of her one-time prosperity.

Italy's third reason for insisting on the cession of Fiume is political, and, because it is based on a deep-seated and haunting fear, it is, perhaps, the most compelling reason of all. Italy does not trust the Jugoslavs. She cannot forget that the Austrian and Hungarian fractions of the new Jugoslav people—in other words, the Slovenes and Croats—were the most faithful subjects of the Dual Monarchy, fighting for the Hapsburgs with a ferocity and determination hardly surpassed in the war. Unlike the Poles and Czecho-Slovaks, who threw in their lot with the Allies, the Slovenes and Croats fought, and fought desperately, for the triumph of the Central Empires. Had these two peoples turned against their masters early in the war, the great struggle would have ended months, perhaps years, earlier than it did. Yet, within a few days after the signing of the Armistice, they became Jugoslavs, and announced that they have always been at heart friendly to the Allies. But, so the Italians argue, their conversion has been too sudden: they have changed their flag but not their hearts; their real allegiance is not to Belgrade but to Berlin. The Italian attitude toward these peoples who have so abruptly switched from enemies to allies is that of the American soldier for the Filipino:

> "He may be a brother of William H. Taft,
> But he ain't no brother of mine."

The Italians are convinced that the three peoples who have been so hastily welded into Jugoslavia will, as the result of internal jealousies and dissensions, eventually disintegrate, and that, when the break-up comes, those portions of the new state which formerly belonged to Austria-Hungary will ally themselves with the great Teutonic or, perhaps, Russo-Teutonic, confederation which, most students of European affairs believe, will arise from the ruins of the Central Empires. When that day comes the new power will look with hungering eyes toward the rich markets which fringe the Middle Sea, and what more convenient gateway through which to pour its merchandise—and, perhaps, its fighting men—than Fiume in friendly hands? In order to bar forever this, the sole gateway to the warm water still open to the Hun, the Italians should, they maintain, be made its guardians.

"But," you argue, "suppose Jugoslavia does *not* break up? How can 14,000,000 Slavs seriously menace Italy's 40,000,000?"

Ah! Now you touch the very heart of the whole matter; now you have put your finger on the secret fear which has animated Italy throughout the controversy over Fiume and Dalmatia. For I do not believe that it is a reincarnated Germany which Italy dreads. It is something far more ominous, more terrifying than that, which alarms her. For, looking across the Adriatic, she sees the monstrous vision of a united and aggressive Slavdom, untold millions strong, of which the Jugoslavs are but the skirmish-line, ready to dispute not merely Italy's schemes for the commercial mastery of the Balkans but her overlordship of that sea which she regards as an Italian lake.

Jugoslavia's claims to Fiume are more briefly stated. Firstly, she lays title to it on the ground that geographically Fiume belongs to Croatia, and that Croatia is now a part of Jugoslavia, or, to give the new country its correct name, the Kingdom of the Serbs, Croats, and Slovenes. This claim is, I think, well founded, and this despite the fact that Italy has attempted to prove, by means of innumerable pamphlets and maps, that Fiume, being within the great semi-circular wall formed by the Alps, is physically Italian. The Jugoslavs demand Fiume, secondly, because, they assert, if Fiume and Sussak are considered as a single city, that city has more Slavs than Italians, while the population of the hinterland is almost solidly Croatian. With the first half of this claim I cannot agree. As I have already pointed out, Sussak is not, and never has been, a part of Fiume, and its annexation is not demanded by the Italians. Conceding, however, for the sake of argument, that Fiume and Sussak are parts of the same city, the most reliable figures which I have been able to obtain show that, even were the Slav majority in Sussak added to the Slav minority in Fiume, the Slavs would still be able to muster barely more than a third of the total population. By far the strongest title which the Slavs have to the city, and the one which commands for them the greatest sympathy, is their assertion that Fiume is the natural and, indeed, almost the only practicable commercial outlet for Jugoslavia, and that the struggling young state needs it desperately. In reply to this, the Italians point out that there are numerous harbors along the Dalmatian coast which would answer the needs of Jugoslavia as well, or almost as well, as Fiume. Now, I am speaking from first-hand knowledge when I assert that this is not so, for I have seen with my own eyes every harbor, or potential harbor, on the eastern coast of the Adriatic from Istria to Greece. As a matter of fact, the entire coast of Dalmatia would not make up to the Jugoslavs for the loss of Fiume. The map gives no idea of the city's importance as the southernmost point at which a standard-gauge railway reaches the Adriatic, for the railway leading to Ragusa, to which the Italians so repeatedly refer as providing an outlet for Jugoslavia, is not only narrow-gauge but is in part a rack-and-pinion mountain line. The situation is best summed up by the commander of the American war-ship on which I dined at Spalato.

"It is not a question of finding a good harbor for the Jugoslavs," he said. "This coast is rich in splendid harbors. It is a question, rather, of finding a practicable route for a standard-gauge railway over or through the mile-high range of the Dinaric Alps, which parallel the entire coast, shutting the coast towns off from the hinterland. Until such a railway is built, the peoples of the interior have no means of getting their products down to the coast save through Fiume. Italy already has the great port of Trieste. Were she also to be awarded Fiume she would have a strangle-hold on the trade of Jugoslavia which would probably mean that country's commercial ruin."

I have now given you, as fairly as I know how, the principal arguments of the rival claimants. The Italians of Fiume, as I have already shown, outnumber the Slavs almost three to one, and it is they who are demanding so violently that the city should be annexed to Italy on the ground of self-determination. But I do not believe that, because there is an undoubted Italian majority in Fiume, the city should be awarded to Italy. If Italy were asking only what was beyond all shadow of question Italian, I should sympathize with her unreservedly. But to place 10,000 Slavs under Italian rule would be as unjust and as provocative of future trouble as to place 30,000 Italians under the rule of Belgrade. Nor is the cession of the city itself the end of Italy's claims, for, in order to place it beyond the range of the enemy's guns (by the "enemy" she means her late allies, the Serbs), in order to maintain control of the railways entering the city, and in order to bring the city actually within her territorial borders, she desires to extend her rule over other thousands of people who are not Italian, who do not speak the Italian tongue, and who do not wish Italian rule. Italy has no stancher friend than I, but neither my profound admiration for what she achieved during the war nor my deep sympathy for the staggering losses she suffered can blind me to the unwisdom, let us call it, of certain of her demands. I am convinced that, when the passions aroused by the controversy have had time to cool, the Italians will themselves question the wisdom of accumulating for themselves future troubles by creating new lost provinces and a new Irredenta by annexing against their will thousands of people of an alien race. Viewing the question from the standpoints of abstract justice, of sound politics, and of common sense, I do not believe that Fiume should be given either to the Italians or to the Jugoslavs, but that the interests of both, as well as the prosperity of the Fumani themselves, should be safeguarded by making it a free city under international control.

No account of the extraordinary drama—farce would be a better name were its possibilities not so tragic—which is being staged at Fiume would be complete without some mention of the romantic figure who is playing the part of hero or villain, according to whether your sympathies are with the Italians or the Jugoslavs. There is nothing romantic, mind you, in Gabriele d'Annunzio's personal appearance. On the contrary, he is one of the most unimpressive-looking men I have ever seen. He is short of stature—not over five feet five, I should guess—and even his beautifully cut clothes, which fit so faultlessly about the waist and hips as to suggest the use of stays, but partially camouflage the corpulency of middle age. His head looks like a new-laid egg which has been highly varnished; his pointed beard is clipped in a fashion which reminded me of the bronze satyrs in the Naples museum; a monocle, worn without a cord, conceals his dead eye, which he lost in battle. His walk is a combination of a mince and a swagger; his movements are those of an actor who knows that the spotlight is upon him.

THE INHABITANTS OF FIUME CHEERING D'ANNUNZIO AND HIS RAIDERS
"Save only Barcelona, Fiume has the most excitable population of any place that I know."
The patron saint of the city is, appropriately enough, St. Vitus

Though d'Annunzio takes high rank among the modern poets, many of his admirers holding him to be the greatest one alive, he is a far greater orator. His diction is perfect, his wealth of imagery exhaustless; I have seen him sway a vast audience as a wheat-field is swayed by the wind. His life he values not at all; the four rows of ribbons which on the breast of his uniform make a splotch of color were not won by his verses. Though well past the half-century mark, he has participated in a score of aerial combats, occupying the observer's seat in his fighting Sva and operating the machine-gun. But perhaps the most brilliant of his military exploits was a bloodless one, when he flew over Vienna and bombed that city with proclamations, written by himself, pointing out to the Viennese the futility of further resistance. His popularity among all classes is amazing; his word is law to the great organization known as the *Combatenti*, composed of the 5,000,000 men who fought in the Italian armies. He is a jingo of the jingoes, his plans for Italian expansion reaching far beyond the annexation of Fiume or even all of Dalmatia, for he has said again and again that he dreams of that day when Italy will have extended her rule over all that territory which once was held by Rome.

He is a very picturesque and interesting figure, is Gabriele d'Annunzio—very much in earnest, wholly sincere, but fanatical, egotistical, intolerant of the rights or opinions of others, a visionary, and perhaps a little mad. I imagine that he would rather have his name linked with that of that other soldier-poet, who "flamed away at Missolonghi" nearly a century ago, than with any other character in history save Garibaldi. D'Annunzio, like Byron, was an exile from his native land. Both had a habit of never paying their bills; both had offended against the social codes of their times; both flamed against what they believed to be injustice and tyranny; both had a passionate love for liberty; both possessed a highly developed sense of the dramatic and delighted in playing romantic rôles. I have heard it said that d'Annunzio's raid on Fiume would make his name immortal, but I doubt it. Barely a score of years have passed since the raid on Johannesburg, which was a far more daring and hazardous exploit than d'Annunzio's Fiume performance, yet to-day how many people remember Doctor Jameson? It can be said for this middle-aged poet that he has successfully defied the government of Italy, that he flouted the royal duke who was sent to parley with him, that he seduced the Italian army and navy into committing open mutiny—"a breach of that military discipline," in the words of the Prime Minister, "which is the foundation of the safety of the state"—and that he has done more to shake foreign confidence in the stability of the Italian character and the dependability of the Italian soldier than the Austro-Germans did when they brought about the disaster at Caporetto.

I have heard it said that the Nitti government had advance knowledge of the raid on Fiume and that the reason it took no vigorous measures against the filibusters was because it secretly approved of their action. This I do not believe. With President Wilson, the Jugoslavs, d'Annunzio, and the Italian army and navy arrayed against him, I am convinced that Mr. Nitti did everything that could be done without precipitating either a war or a revolution. Much credit is also due to the Jugoslavs for their forbearance and restraint under great provocation. They must have been sorely tempted to give the Poet the spanking he so richly deserves.

When the small army of newspaper correspondents who were despatched by the great New York and London dailies to Khartoum to interview Colonel Roosevelt upon his emergence from the jungle started up the White Nile to meet the explorer, they were deterred, both by the shortage of boats and the question of expense, from chartering individual steamers. But the public at home was not permitted to know of these petty limitations and annoyances. On the contrary, people all over the United States, at their breakfast-tables, read the despatches from the far-off Sudan dated from "On board the New York *Herald's* dahabeah *Rameses*" or "The New York *American's* despatch-boat *Abbas Hilmi,*" or "The Chicago *Tribune's* special steamer *General Gordon,*" and never dreamed that the young men in sun-helmets and white linen who were writing those despatches were comfortably seated under the awnings of the same decrepit stern-wheeler, which they had chartered jointly, but on which, in order to lend importance and dignity to his despatches, each correspondent had bestowed a particular name.

But the destroyer *Sirio,* which we found awaiting us at Fiume, we did not have to share with any one. Thanks to the courtesy of the Italian Ministry of Marine, she was all ours, while we were aboard her, from her knife-like prow to the screws kicking the water under her stern.

"I am under orders to place myself entirely at your disposal," explained her youthful and very stiffly starched skipper,

Commander Poggi. "I am to go where you desire and to stop as long as you please. Those are my instructions."

Thus it came about that, shortly after noon on a scorching summer day, we cast off our moorings and, leaving quarrel-torn Fiume abaft, turned the nose of the *Sirio* sou' by sou'-west, down the coast of Dalmatia. The sun-kissed waters of the Bay of Quarnero looked for all the world like a vast azure carpet strewn with a million sparkling diamonds; on our starboard quarter stretched the green-clad slopes of Istria, with the white villas of Abbazia peeping coyly out from amid the groves of pine and laurel; to the eastward the bleak brown peaks of the Dinaric Alps rose, savage, mysterious, forbidding, against the cloudless summer sky. Perhaps no stretch of coast in all the world has had so varied and romantic a history or so many masters as this Dalmatian seaboard. Since the days of the tattooed barbarians who called themselves Illyrian, this coast has been ruled in turn by Phœnicians, Celts, Macedonians, Greeks, Romans, Goths, Byzantines, Croats, Serbs, Bulgars, Huns, Avars, Saracens, Normans, Magyars, Genoese, Venetians, Tartars, Bosnians, Turks, French, Russians, Montenegrins, British, Austrians, Italians—and now by Americans, for from Cape Planca southward to Ragusa, a distance of something over a hundred miles, the United States is the governing power and an American admiral holds undisputed sway.

Leaning over the rail as we fled southward I lost myself in dreams of far-off days. In my mind I could see, sweeping past in imaginary review, those other vessels which, all down the ages, had skirted these same shores: the purple sails of Phœnicia, Greek galleys bearing colonists from Cnidus, Roman triremes with the slaves sweating at the oars, high-powered, low-waisted Norman caravels with the arms of their marauding masters painted on their bellowing canvas, stately Venetian carracks with carved and gilded sterns, swift-sailing Uskok pirate craft, their decks crowded with swarthy men in skirts and turbans, Genoese galleons, laden with the products of the hot lands, French and English frigates with brass cannon peering from their rows of ports, the grim, gray monsters of the Hapsburg navy. And then I suddenly awoke, for, coming up from the southward at full speed, their slanting funnels vomiting great clouds of smoke, were four long, low, lean, incredibly swift craft, ostrich-plumes of snowy foam curling from their bows, which sped past us like wolfhounds running with their noses to the ground. As they passed I could see quite plainly, flaunting from each taffrail, a flag of stripes and stars.

The sun was sinking behind Italy when, threading our way amid the maze of islands and islets which border the Dalmatian shore, we saw beyond our bows, silhouetted against the rose-coral of the evening sky, the slender campaniles and the crenellated ramparts of Zara. It was so still and calm and beautiful that I felt as though I were looking at a scene upon a stage and that the curtain would descend at any moment and destroy the illusion. The little group of white-clad naval officers who greeted us upon the quay informed us that the governor-general, Admiral Count Millo, had placed at our disposal the yacht *Zara*, formerly the property of the Austrian Emperor, on which we were to live during our stay in the Dalmatian capital. It was a peculiarly thoughtful thing to do, for the summers are hot in Zara, the city's few hotels leave much to be desired, and a stay at a palace, even that of a provincial governor, is hedged about by a certain amount of formality and restrictions. But the *Zara*, while we were aboard her, was as much ours as the *Mayflower* is Mr. Wilson's. We occupied the spacious after-cabins, exquisitely paneled in white mahogany, which had been used by the Austrian archduchesses and whose furnishings still bore the imperial crown, and our breakfasts were served under the white awnings stretched over the after-deck, where, lounging in the grateful shade, we could look out across the harbor, dotted with the gaudy sails of fishing craft and bordered by the walls and gardens of the quaint old city, to the islands of Arbe and Pago, rising, like huge, uncut emeralds, from the lazy southern sea. At noon we usually lunched with a score or more of staff-officers in the large, cool dining-room of the officers' mess, and at night we dined with the governor-general and his family at the palace, formerly the residence of the Austrian viceroys. Dinner over, we lounged in cane chairs on the terrace, served by white-clad, silent-footed servants with coffee, cigarettes, and the maraschino for which this coast is famous. Those were never-to-be-forgotten evenings, for the gently heaving breast of the Adriatic glowed with a phosphorescent luminousness, the air was heavy with the fragrance of orange, almond, and oleander, the sky was like purple velvet, and the stars seemed very near.

Though the population of Dalmatia is overwhelmingly Slav, quite two-thirds of the 14,000 inhabitants of Zara, its capital, are Italian. Yet, were it not for the occasional Morlachs in their picturesque costumes seen in the markets or on the wharfs, one would not suspect the presence of any Slav element in the town, for the dim and tortuous streets and the spacious squares bear Italian names— Via del Duomo, Riva Vecchia, Piazza della Colonna; crouching above the city gates is the snarling Lion of St. Mark, and everywhere one hears the liquid accents of the Latin. Zara, like Fiume, is an Italian colony set down on a Slavonian shore, and, like its sister-city to the north, it bears the indelible and unmistakable imprint of Italian civilization.

The long, narrow strip of territory sandwiched between the Adriatic and the Dinaric Alps which comprised the Austrian province of Dalmatia, though upward of 200 miles in length, has an area scarcely greater than that of Connecticut and a population smaller than that of Cleveland. Scarcely more than a tenth of its whole surface is under the plow, the rest, where it is not altogether sterile, consisting of mountain pasture. With the exception of scattered groves on the landward slopes, the country is virtually treeless, the forests for which Dalmatia was once famous having been cut down by the Venetian ship-builders or wantonly burned by the Uskok pirates, while every attempt at replanting has been frustrated by the shallowness of the soil, the frequent droughts, and the multitudes of goats which browse on the young trees. The dreary expanse of the Bukovica, lying between Zara and the Bosnian frontier, is, without exception, the most inhospitable region that I have ever seen. For mile after mile, far as the eye can see, the earth is overlaid by a thick stratum of jagged limestone, so rough that no horse could traverse it, so sharp and flinty that a quarter of an hour's walking across it would cut to pieces the stoutest pair of boots. Under the rays of the summer sun these rocks become as hot as the top of a stove; so hot, indeed, that eggs can be cooked upon them, while metal objects exposed for only a few minutes to the sun will burn the hand. Scattered here and there over this terrible plateau are tiny farmsteads, their houses and the walls shutting in the little patches under cultivation being built from the stones obtained in clearing the soil, a task requiring incredible patience. No wonder that the folk who dwell in them are characterized by expressions as stony and hopeless as the soil from which they wring a wretched existence.

No seaboard of the Mediterranean, save only the coast of Greece, is so deeply indented as the Dalmatian littoral, with Its unending succession of rock-bound bays, as frequent as the perforations on a postage-stamp, and its thick fringe of islands. In calm weather the channels between these islands and the mainland resemble a chain of landlocked lakes, like those in the Adirondacks or in southern Ontario, being connected by narrow straits called *canales*, brilliantly clear to a depth of several fathoms. As a rule, the surrounding hills are rugged, bleached yellow or pale russet, and destitute of verdure, but their monotony is relieved by the half-ruined castles and monasteries which, perched on the rocky heights, perpetually reminded me of Howard Pyle's paintings, and by the medieval charm of Zara, Sebenico, Spalato, Ragusa, Arbe, and Curzola, whose architecture, though predominantly Venetian, bears characteristic traces of the many races which have ruled them.

Just as Italy insisted on pushing her new borders up to the Brenner so that she might have a strategic frontier on the north, so she lays claim to the larger of the Dalmatian islands—Lissa, Lésina, Curzola, and certain others—in order to protect her Adriatic shores. A glance at the map will make her reasons amply plain. There stretches Italy's eastern coastline, 600 miles of it, from Venice to Otranto, with half a dozen busy cities and a score of fishing towns, as bare and unprotected as a bald man's hatless head. Not only is there not a single naval base on Italy's Adriatic coast south of Venice, but there is no harbor or inlet that can be transformed into one. Yet across the Adriatic, barely four hours steam by destroyer away, is a wilderness of islands and deep harbors where an enemy's fleet could lie safely hidden, from which it could emerge to attack Italian commerce or to bombard Italy's unprotected coast towns, and where it could take refuge when the pursuit became too hot. All down the ages the dwellers along Italy's eastern seaboard have been terrorized by naval raids from across the Adriatic. And Italy has determined that they shall be terrorized no more. How history repeats itself! Just as Rome, twenty-two centuries ago, could not permit the neighboring islands of Sicily to fall into the hands of Carthage, so Italy cannot permit these coastwise islands, which form her only protection against attacks from the east, to pass under the control of the Jugoslavs.

"But," I said to the Italians with whom I discussed the matter, "why do you need any such protection now that the world is to have a League of Nations? Isn't that a sufficient guarantee that the Jugoslavs will never attack you?"

"The League of Nations is in theory a splendid thing," was their answer. "We subscribe to it in principle most heartily. But because there is a policeman on duty in your street, do you leave wide open your front door?"

To be quite candid, I do not think that it is against Jugoslavia, or, perhaps it would be more accurate to say, against an unaided Jugoslavia, that Italy is taking precautions. I have already said, I believe, that thinking Italians look with grave forebodings to the day when a great Slav confederation shall rise across the Adriatic, but that day, as they know full well, is still far distant. Italy's desperate insistence on retaining possession of the more important Dalmatian islands is dictated by a far more immediate danger than that. She is convinced that her next war will be fought, not with the weak young state of Jugoslavia, but with Jugoslavia *allied with France*. Every Italian with whom I discussed the question—and I might add, without boasting, many highly placed and well-informed Italians have honored me with their confidence—firmly believes that France is jealous of Italy's rapidly increasing power in the Mediterranean, and that she is secretly intriguing with the Jugoslavs and the Greeks to prevent Italy obtaining commercial supremacy in the Balkans. I do not say that this is my opinion, mind you, but I do say that it is the opinion held by most Italians. I found that the resentment against the French for what the Italians term France's "betrayal" of Italy at the Peace Conference was almost universal; everywhere in Italy I found a deep-seated distrust of France's commercial ambitions and political designs. Though the Italians admit that the Jugoslavs will not be able to build a navy for many years to come, they fear, or profess to fear, that the day is not immeasurably far distant when a French battle fleet, co-operating with the armies of Jugoslavia, will threaten Italy's Adriatic seaboard. And they are determined that, should such a day ever come, French ships shall not be afforded the protection, as were the Austrian, of the Dalmatian islands. Italy, with her great modern battle fleet and her 5,000,000 fighting men, regards the threats of Jugoslavia with something akin to contempt, but France, turned imperialistic and arrogant by her victory over the Hun, Italy distrusts and fears, believing that, while protesting her friendship, she is secretly fomenting opposition to legitimate Italian aspirations in the Balkan peninsula and in the Middle Sea. (Again let me remind you that I am giving you not my own, but Italy's point of view.) You will sneer at this, perhaps, as a phantasm of the imagination, but I assure you, with all the earnestness and emphasis at my command, that this distrust of one great Latin nation for another, whether it is justified or not, forms a deadly menace to the future peace of the world.

Because I did not wish to confine my observations to the coast towns, which are, after all, essentially Italian, I motored across Dalmatia at its widest part, from Zara, through Benkovac, Kistonje, and Knin, to the little hamlet of Kievo, on the Jugoslav frontier. Though the Slav population of the Dalmatian hinterland is, according to the assertions of Belgrade, bitterly hostile to Italian rule, I did not detect a single symptom of animosity toward the Italian officers who were my companions on the part of the peasants whom we passed. They displayed, on the contrary, the utmost courtesy and good feeling, the women, looking like huge and gaudily dressed dolls in their snowy blouses and embroidered aprons, courtesying, while the tall, fine-looking men gravely touched the little round caps which are the national head-gear of Dalmatia.

Kievo is the last town in Dalmatia, being only a few score yards from the Bosnian frontier. Its little garrison was in command of a young Italian captain, a tall, slender fellow with the blond beard of a Viking and the dreamy eyes of a poet. He had been stationed at this lonely outpost for seven months, he told me, and he welcomed us as a man wrecked on a desert island would welcome a rescue party. In order to escape from the heat and filth and insects of the village, he had built in a near-by grove a sort of arbor, with a roof of interlaced branches to keep off the sun. Its furnishings consisted of a home-made table, an army cot, two or three decrepit chairs, and a phonograph. I did not need to inquire where he had obtained the phonograph, for on its cover was stenciled the familiar red triangle of the Y.M.C.A.—the *"Yimka,"* as the Italians call it—which operates more than 300 *casas* for the use of the Italian army. While our host was preparing a dubious-looking drink from sweet, bright-colored syrups and lukewarm water, I amused myself by glancing over the little stack of records on the table. They were, of course, nearly all Italian, but I came upon three that I knew well: *"Loch Lomond," "Old Folks at Home"* and *"So Long, Letty."* It was like meeting a party of old friends in a strange land. I tried the later record, and though it was not very clear, for the captain's supply of needles had run out and he had been reduced to using ordinary pins, it was startling to hear Charlotte Greenwood's familiar voice caroling *"So long, so long, Letty,"* there on the borders of Bosnia, with a picket of curious Jugoslavs, rifles across their knees, seated on the rocky hillside, barely a stone's throw away. Still, come to think about it, the war produced many contrasts quite as strange, as, for example, when the New York Irish, the old 69th, crossed the Rhine with the regimental band playing *"The Sidewalks of New York."*

We touched at Sebenico, which is forty knots down the coast from Zara, in order to accept an invitation to lunch with Lieutenant-General Montanari, who commands all the Italian troops in Dalmatia. Now before we started down the Adriatic we had been warned that, because of President Wilson's attitude on the Fiume question, the feeling against Americans ran very high, and that from the Italians we must be prepared for coldness, if not for actual insults. Well, this luncheon at Sebenico was an example of the insults we received and the coldness with which we were treated. Because our destroyer was late, half a hundred busy officers delayed their midday meal for two hours in order not to sit down without us. The table was decorated with American flags, and other American flags had been hand-painted on the menus. And, as a final affront, a destroyer had been sent across the Adriatic Sea to obtain lobsters because the general had heard that my wife was particularly fond of them. After that experience don't talk to me about Southern hospitality. Though the Italians bitterly resent President Wilson's interference in an affair which they consider peculiarly their own, their resentment does not extend to the President's countrymen. Their attitude is aptly illustrated by an incident which took place at the mess of a famous regiment of Bersaglieri, when the picture of President Wilson, which had hung on the wall of the mess-hall, opposite that of the King, was taken down—and an American flag hung in its place.

The most interesting building in Sebenico is the cathedral, which was begun when America had yet to be discovered. The chief glory of the cathedral is its exterior, with its superb carved doors, its countless leering, grinning gargoyles—said to represent the evil spirits expelled from the church—and a broad frieze, running entirely around the edifice, composed of sculptured likenesses of the architects, artists, sculptors, masons, and master-builders who participated in its construction. Put collars, neckties, and derby hats on some of them and you would have striking likenesses of certain labor leaders of to-day. The next time a building of note is erected in this country the countenances of the bricklayers, hod-carriers, and walking delegates might be immortalized in some such fashion. I offer the suggestion to the labor-unions for what it is worth.

Throughout all the years of Austrian domination the citizens of Sebenico remained loyal to their Italian traditions, as is proved by the medallions ornamenting the façade of the cathedral, each of which bears the image of a saint. One of these sculptured saints, it was pointed out to me, has the unmistakable features of Victor Emanuel I, another those of Garibaldi. Thus did the Italian workmen of their day cunningly express their defiance of Austria's tyranny by ornamenting one of her most splendid cathedrals with the heads of Italian heroes. Imagine carving the heads of Elihu Root and Charles E. Hughes on the façade of Tammany Hall!

Next to the cathedral, the most interesting building in Sebenico is the insect-powder factory. It is a large factory and does a thriving business, the need for its product being Balkan-wide. If, for upward of five months, you had fought nightly engagements with the *cimex lectularius*, you would understand how vital is an ample supply of powder. Believe me or not, as you please, but in many parts of Dalmatia and Albania we were compelled to defend our beds against nocturnal raiding-parties by raising veritable ramparts of insect-powder, very much as in Flanders we threw up earthworks against the assaults of the Hun, while in Monastir the only known way of obtaining sleep is to set the legs of one's bed in basins filled with kerosene.

Four hours steaming south from Sebenico brought us to Spalato, the largest city of Dalmatia and one of the most picturesquely situated towns in the Levant. It owes its name to the great palace (*palatium*) of Diocletian, within the precincts of which a great part of the old town is built and around which have sprung up its more modern suburbs. Cosily ensconced between the stately marble columns which formed the palace's façade are fruit, tobacco, barber, shoe, and tailor shops, whose proprietors drive a roaring trade with the sailors from the international armada assembled in the harbor. A great hall, which had probably originally been one of the vestibules of the palace, was occupied by the Knights of Columbus, the place being in charge of a khaki-clad priest, Father Mullane, of Johnstown, Pa., who twice daily dispensed true American hospitality, in the form of hot doughnuts and mugs of steaming coffee, to the blue-jackets from the American ships. As there was no coal to be had in the town, he made the doughnuts with the aid of a plumber's blowpipe. In the course of our conversation Father Mullane mentioned that he was living with the Serbian bishop—at least I think he was a bishop-of Spalato.

"I suppose he speaks English or French," I remarked.

"He does not," was the answer.

"Then you must have picked up some Serb or Italian," I hazarded.

"Niver a wurrd of thim vulgar tongues do I know," said he.

"Then how do you and the bishop get along?"

"Shure," said Father Mullane, in the rich brogue which is, I imagine, something of an affectation, "an' what is the use of bein' educated for the church if we were not able to converse with ease an' fluency in iligant an' refined Latin?"

The New Frontiers of Freedom: From the Alps to the Aegean

When we were leaving Spalato, Father Mullane presented us with a *Bon Voyage* package which contained cigarettes, a box of milk chocolate, and a five-pound tin of gum-drops. The cigarettes we smoked, the chocolate we ate, but the gum-drops we used for tips right across the Balkans. In lands whose people have not known the taste of sugar for five years we found that a handful of gum-drops would accomplish more than money. A few men with Father Mullane's resource, tact, and sense of humor would do more than all the diplomats under the roof of the Hotel Crillon to settle international differences and make the nations understand each other.

I had been warned by archæological friends, before I went to Dalmatia, that the ruins of Salona, which once was the capital of Roman Dalmatia and the site of the summer palace of Diocletian, would probably disappoint me. They date from the period of Roman decadence, so my learned friends explained, and, though following Roman traditions, frequently show traces of negligence, a fact which is accounted for by the haste with which the ailing and hypochondriac Emperor sought to build himself a retreat from the world. Still, the little excursion—for Salona is only five miles from Spalato—provided much that was worth the seeing: a partially excavated amphitheater, a long row of stone sarcophagi lying in a trench, one or two fine gates, and some beautifully preserved mosaics. I must confess, however, that I was more interested in the modern aspects of this region than in its glorious past, for, standing upon the massive walls of the Roman city, I looked down upon a panorama of power such as Diocletian had never pictured in his wildest dreams, for, moored in a long and impressive row, their stern-lines made fast to the *Molo*, was a line of war-ships flying the flags of England, France, Italy, and the United States. On the right of the line, as befitted the fact that its commander was the senior naval officer and in charge of all this portion of the coast, was Admiral Andrews's flag-ship, the *Olympia*, but little changed, at least to the casual glance, since that day, more than twoscore years ago, when she blazed her way into Manila Bay and won for us a colonial empire. On her bridge, outlined in brass tacks, I was shown Admiral Dewey's footprints, just as he stood at the beginning of the battle when he gave the order "You may fire when you are ready, Gridley."

Of the 18,000 inhabitants of Spalato, less than a tenth are Italian, the general character of the town and the sympathies of its inhabitants being strongly pro-Slav. In fact, its streets were filled with Jugoslav soldiers, many of them still wearing the uniforms of the Austrian regiments in which they had served but with Serbian *képis*, while others looked strangely familiar in khaki uniforms furnished them by the United States. It being warm weather, most of the men wore their coats unbuttoned, thereby displaying a considerable expanse of hairy chest or violently colored underwear and producing a somewhat negligée effect. Because of the presence in the town of the Jugoslav soldiery, the crews of the Italian war-ships were not permitted to go ashore with the sailors of the other nations, as Admiral Andrews feared that their presence might provoke unpleasant incidents. Hence their "shore leave" had, for nearly six months, been confined to the narrow concrete *Molo*, where they were permitted to stroll in the evenings and where the Italian girls of the town came to see them. For a Jugoslav girl to have been seen in company with an Italian sailor would have meant her social ostracism, if nothing worse.

Though Italy will unquestionably insist on the cession of certain of the Dalmatian islands, in order, as I have already pointed out, to assure herself a defensible eastern frontier, and though she will ask for Zara and possibly for Sebenico on the ground of their preponderantly Italian character, I believe that she is prepared to abandon her original claims to Dalmatia, which is, when all is said and done, almost purely Slavonian, Jugoslavia thus obtaining nearly 550 miles of coast. Now I will be quite frank and say that when I went to Dalmatia I was strongly opposed to the extension of Italian rule over that region. And I still believe that it would be a political mistake. But, after seeing the country from end to end and talking with the Italian officials who have been temporarily charged with its administration, I have become convinced that they have the best interests of the people genuinely at heart and that the Dalmatians might do worse, so far as justice and progress are concerned, than to intrust their future to the guidance of such men.

The New Frontiers of Freedom: From the Alps to the Aegean

It had been our original intention to steam straight south from Spalato to the Bocche di Cattaro and Montenegro, but, being foot-loose and free and having plenty of coal in the *Sirio's* bunkers, we decided to make a detour in order to visit the Curzolane Islands. In case you cannot recall its precise situation, I might remind you that the Curzolane Archipelago, consisting of several good-sized islands—Brazza, Lésina, Lissa, Mélida, and Curzola—and a great number of smaller ones, lies off the Dalmatian coast, almost opposite Ragusa. From Spalato we laid our course due south, past Solta, famed for its honey produced from rosemary and the cistus-rose; skirted the wooded shores of Brazza, the largest island of the group, rounded Capo Pellegrino and entered the lovely harbor of Lésina. We did not anchor but, slowing to half-speed, made the circuit of the little port, running close enough to the shore to obtain pictures of the famous Loggia built by Sanmicheli, the Fondazo, the ancient Venetian arsenal, and the crumbling Spanish fort, perched high on a crag above the town. Then south by west again, past Lissa, the western-most island of the group, where an Italian fleet under Persano was defeated and destroyed by an Austrian squadron under Tegetthof in 1866. A marble lion in the local cemetery commemorated the victory and marked the resting-places of the Austrian dead, but when the Italians took possession of the island after the Armistice they changed the inscription on the monument so that it now commemorates their final victory over Austria. It was not, I think, a very sportsmanlike proceeding.

Leaving Lissa to starboard, we steamed through the Canale di Sabbioncello, with exquisite panoramas unrolling on either hand, and dropped anchor off the quay of Curzola, where the governor of the islands, Admiral Piazza, awaited us with his staff. In spite of the bleakness of the surrounding mountains, Curzola is one of the most exquisitely beautiful little towns that I have ever seen. The next time you are in the Adriatic you should not fail to go there. Time and the hand of man—for the people are a color-loving race—have given many tints, soft and bright, to its roofs, towers, and ramparts. It is a town of dim, narrow, winding streets, of steep flights of worn stone steps, of moss-covered archways, and of some of the most splendid specimens of the domestic architecture of the Middle Ages that exist outside of the Street of the Crusaders in Rhodes. The sole modern touches are the costumes of the islanders, and they are sufficiently picturesque not to spoil the picture. How the place has escaped the motion-picture people I fail to understand. (As a matter of fact, it hasn't, for I took with me an operator and a camera—the first the islanders had ever seen.) Besides the Cathedral of San Marco, with its splendid doors, its exquisitely carved choir-stalls black with age and use, its choir balustrade and pulpit of translucent alabaster, and its dim old altar-piece by Tintoretto, the town boasts the Loggia or council chambers, the palace of the Venetian governors, the noble mansion of the Arnieri, and, brooding over all, a towering campanile, five centuries old. The Lion of St. Mark, which appears on several of the public buildings, holds beneath its paw a closed instead of an open book—symbolizing, so I was told, the islanders' dissatisfaction with certain laws of the Venetians.

But the phase of my visit which I enjoyed the most was when Admiral Piazza took us across the bay, on a Detroit-built submarine-chaser, to a Franciscan monastery dating from the fifteenth century. We were met by the abbot at the water-stairs, and, after being shown the beautiful Venetian Gothic cloisters, with alabaster columns whose carving was almost lacelike in its delicate tracery, we were led along a wooded path beside the sea, over a carpet of pine-needles, to a cloistered rose-garden, in which stood, amid a bower of blossoms, a blue and white statue of the Virgin. The fragrance of the flowers in the little enclosure was like the incense in a church, above our heads the great pines formed a canopy of green, and the music was furnished by the birds and the murmuring sea. Here we seemed a world away from the waiting armies and the great gray battleships, from the quarrels of Latin and Slav. It was the first real peace that I had known after five years of war, and I should have liked to remain there longer. But Montenegro, Albania, Macedonia, all the unhappy, war-torn lands of the Near East lay before me, and I turned reluctantly away. But my thoughts keep harking back to the little town beside the turquoise bay, to the restfulness of its old, old buildings, to the perfume of its flowers, and the whispering voice of its turquoise sea. So some day, when the world is really at peace and there are no more wars to write about, I think that I shall go back to where

The New Frontiers of Freedom: From the Alps to the Aegean

"Far, far from here,
The Adriatic breaks in a warm bay
Among the green Illyrian hills."

CHAPTER III

THE CEMETERY OF FOUR EMPIRES

We stood on the forward deck of the *Sirio* as she slipped southward, through the placid waters of the Adriatic, at twenty knots an hour. Less than a league away the Balkan mountains, savage, mysterious, forbidding, rose in a rocky rampart against the eastern sky.

"Did it ever occur to you," remarked the Italian officer who stood beside me, a noted historian in his own land, "that four great empires have died as a result of their lust for domination over the wretched lands which lie beyond those mountains? Austria coveted Serbia—and the empire of the Hapsburgs is in fragments now. Russia, seeing her influence in the peninsula imperiled, hastened to the support of her fellow Slavs—but Russia has gone down in red ruin, and the Romanoffs are dead. Germany, seeking a gateway to the warm water, and a highway to the East, seized on the excuse thus offered to launch her waiting armies—and the empire reared by the Hohenzollerns is bankrupt and broken. Turkey fought to retain her hold on such European territory as still remained under the crescent banner. To-day a postmortem is about to be held on the Turkish Empire and the House of Osman. Think of it! Four great empires, four ancient dynasties, lie buried over there in the Balkans. It is something more than a range of mountains at which we are looking; it is the wall of a cemetery."

Rada di Antivari is a U-shaped bay, the color of a turquoise, from whose shores the Montenegrin mountains rise in tiers, like the seats of an arena. We put in there unexpectedly because a *bora*, sweeping suddenly down from the northwest, had lashed the Adriatic into an ugly mood and our destroyer, whose decks were almost as near the water as those of a submarine running awash, was not a craft that one would choose for comfort in such weather. Nor was our feeling of security increased by the knowledge that we were skirting the edges of one of the largest mine-fields in the Adriatic. But the *Sirio* had scarcely poked her sharp nose around the end of the breakwater which provides the excuse for dignifying the exposed roadstead of Antivari (with the accent on the second syllable, so that it rhymes with "discovery") by the name of harbor before I saw what we had stumbled upon some form of trouble. There were three other Italian destroyers in the harbor but, instead of being moored snugly alongside the quay, they were strung out in a semblance of battle formation, so that their deck-guns, from which the canvas muzzle-covers had been removed, could sweep the rocky heights above and around them. A string of signal-flags broke out from our masthead and was answered in like fashion by the flag-ship of the flotilla, after which formal exchange of greetings our wireless began to crackle and splutter in an animated explanation of our unexpected appearance. Our hawsers had scarcely been made fast before a launch left the flag-ship and came plowing toward us, a knot of white-uniformed officers in the stern. From the blue rug with the Italian arms, which, as I could see through my glasses, was draped over the stern-sheets, I deduced that the commander of the flotilla was paying us a visit.

"You have come at rather an unfortunate moment," he said after the introductions were over. "Last night we were fired on by Jugoslavs on the mountainside over there," indicating the heights across the harbor. "In fact, the firing has just ceased. There must have been a thousand of them or more, judging from the flashes. But I hope that madame will not be alarmed, for she is really quite safe. They are firing at long range, and the only danger is from a stray bullet. Still, it is most embarrassing. On madame's account I am sorry."

His manner was that of a host apologizing to a guest because the children of the family have measles and at the same time attempting to convince the guest that measles are hardly ever contagious. I relieved his quite obvious embarrassment by assuring him that Mrs. Powell much preferred taking chances with snipers' bullets to the discomfort of a destroyer in an ugly sea; and that, having journeyed six thousand miles for the express purpose of seeing what was happening in the Balkans, we would be disappointed if nothing happened at all.

The New Frontiers of Freedom: From the Alps to the Aegean

When I left Paris for the Adriatic I carried with me the impression, as the result of conversations with members of the various peace delegations, that the people of Montenegro were almost unanimously in favor of annexation to Serbia, thereby becoming a part of the new Kingdom of the Serbs, Croats, and Slovenes. But before I had spent twenty-four hours in Montenegro itself I discovered that on the subject of the political future of their little country the Montenegrins are very far from being of the same mind. And, being a simple, primitive folk, and strong believers in the superiority of the bullet to the ballot, instead of sitting down and arguing the matter, they take cover behind a convenient rock and, when their political opponents pass by, take pot-shots at them.

My preconceived opinions about political conditions in Montenegro were largely based on the knowledge that shortly after the signing of the Armistice a Montenegrin National Assembly, so called, had met at Podgoritza, and, after declaring itself in favor of the deposition of King Nicholas and the Petrovitch dynasty, which has ruled in Montenegro since William of Orange sat on the throne of England, voted for the union of Montenegro with the Kingdom of the Serbs, Croats, and Slovenes. Just how representative of the real sentiments of the nation was this assembly I do not know, but that the sentiment in favor of such a surrender of Montenegrin independence is far from being overwhelming would seem to be proved by the fact that the Serbs, in order to hold the territory thus given to them, have found it necessary to install a Serbian military governor in Cetinje, to replace by Serbs all the Montenegrin prefects, to raise a special gendarmerie recruited from men who are known to be friendly to Serbia and officered by Serbs, and to occupy this sister-state, which, it is alleged, requested union with Serbia of its own free will, with two battalions of Serbian infantry. If Montenegrin sentiment for the union is as overwhelming as Belgrade claims, then it seems to me that the Serbs are acting in a rather high-handed fashion.

I talked with a good many people while I was in Montenegro, and I was especially careful not to meet them through the medium of either Serbs or Italians. From these conversations I learned that the Montenegrins are divided into three factions. The first of these, and the smallest, desires the return of the King. It represents the old

The New Frontiers of Freedom: From the Alps to the Aegean

conservative element and is composed of the men who have fought under him in many wars. The second faction, which is the noisiest and at present holds the reins of power, advocates the annexation of Montenegro to Serbia and the deposition of King Nicholas in favor of the Serbian Prince-Regent Alexander. The third party, which, though it has no means of making its desires known, is, I am inclined to believe, the largest, and which numbers among its supporters the most level-headed and far-seeing men in the country, while frankly distrustful of Serbian ambitions and unwilling to submit to Serbian dictatorship, possesses sufficient vision to recognize the political and commercial advantages which would accrue to Montenegro were she to become an equal partner in a confederation of those Jugoslav countries which claim the same racial origin. Most thoughtful Montenegrins have always been in favor of a union of all the southern Slavs, along the general lines, perhaps, of the Germanic Confederation, but this must not be interpreted as implying that they are in favor of a union merely of Montenegro with Serbia, which would mean the absorption of the smaller country by the larger one. They are determined that, if such a confederation is brought about, Serbia shall not occupy the dictatorial position which Prussia did in Germany, and that the Karageorgevitches shall not play a rôle analogous to that of the Hohenzollerns. Montenegro, remember, threw off the Turkish yoke a century and three-quarters before Serbia was able to achieve her liberty, and the patriotic among her people feel that this hard-won, long-held independence should not lightly be thrown away.

It is not generally known, perhaps, that, when Austria declared war on Serbia in August, 1914, an offensive and defensive alliance already existed between Serbia, Greece, and Montenegro. We know how highly Greece valued her signature to that treaty. Montenegro, with an area two-thirds that of New Jersey, and a population less than that of Milwaukee, could easily have used her weakness as an excuse for standing aside, like Greece. Very likely Austria would not have molested her and the little country would have been spared the horrors of a third war within two years. But King Nicholas's conception of what constituted loyalty and honor was different from Constantine's. Instead of accepting the extensive territorial compensations offered by the Austrian envoy if Montenegro would remain neutral, King Nicholas wired to the Serbian Premier, M. Pachitch: *"Serbia may rely on the brotherly and unconditional support of Montenegro in this moment, on which depends the fate of the Serbian nation, as well as on any other occasion,"* and took the field at the head of 40,000 troops—all the men able to bear arms in the little kingdom.

It has been repeatedly asserted by his enemies that King Nicholas sold out to the Austrians and that, therefore, he deserves neither sympathy nor consideration. As to this I have no *direct* knowledge. How could I? But, after talking with nearly all of the leading actors in the Montenegrin drama, it is my personal belief that the King, though guilty of many indiscretions and errors of policy, did not betray his people. I am not ignorant of the King's shortcomings in other respects. But in this case I believe that he has been grossly maligned. If he did sell out he drove an extremely poor bargain, for he is living in exile, in extremely straitened circumstances, his only luxury a car which the French Government loans him. It is difficult to believe that, had he been a traitor to the Allied cause, the British, French, and Italian governments would continue to recognize him, to pay him subventions, and to treat him as a ruling sovereign. Certain American diplomats have told me that they were convinced that the King had a secret understanding with Austria, though they admitted quite frankly that their convictions were based on suspicions which they could not prove. To offset this, a very exalted personage, whose name for obvious reasons I cannot mention, but whose integrity and whose sources of information are beyond question, has given me his word that, to his personal knowledge, Nicholas had neither a treaty nor a secret understanding with the enemy.

"The propaganda against him had been so insidious and successful, however," my informant concluded, "that even his own soldiers were convinced that he had sold out to Austria and when the King attempted to rally them as they were falling back from the positions on Mount Lovtchen they jeered in his face, shouting that he had betrayed them. Yet I, who was on the spot and who am familiar with all the facts, give you my personal assurance that he had not."

The New Frontiers of Freedom: From the Alps to the Aegean

Nor did the King give up his sword to the Austrian commander at Grahovo, as was reported in the European press. When, with three-quarters of his country overrun by the Austrians, his chief of staff, Colonel Pierre Pechitch of the Serbian Army, reported *"Henceforth all resistance and all fighting against the enemy is impossible. There is no chance of the situation improving,"* King Nicholas, in the words of Baron Sonnino, then Italian Foreign Minister, "preferred to withdraw into exile rather than sign a separate peace."

I may be wrong in my conclusions, of course; the cabinet ministers and the ambassadors and the generals in whose honor and truthfulness I believe may have deliberately deceived me, but, after a most painstaking and conscientious investigation, I am convinced that we have been misinformed and blinded by a propaganda against King Nicholas and his people which has rarely been equaled in audacity of untruth and dexterity of misrepresentation. To employ the methods used by certain Balkan politicians in their attempted elimination of Montenegro as an independent nation even Tammany Hall would be ashamed.

When, upon the occupation of Montenegro by the Austrians, the King fled to France and established his government at Neuilly, near Paris—just as the fugitive Serbian Government was established at Corfu and the Belgian at Le Havre—England, France, and Italy entered into an agreement to pay him a subvention, for the maintenance of himself and his government, until such time as the status of Montenegro was definitely settled by the Peace Conference. England ceased paying her share of this subvention early in the spring of 1919. When, a few weeks later, it was announced that King Nicholas was preparing to go to Italy to visit his daughter, Queen Elena, the French Minister to the court of Montenegro bluntly informed him that the French Government regarded his proposed visit to Italy as the first step toward his return to Montenegro, and that, should he cross the French frontier, France would immediately break off diplomatic relations with Montenegro and cease paying her share of the subvention. This would seem to bear out the assertion, which I heard everywhere in the Balkans, that France is bending every effort toward building up a strong Jugoslavia in order to offset Italy's territorial and commercial ambitions in the peninsula. The

French indignantly repudiate the suggestion that they are coercing the Montenegrin King.

"How absurd!" exclaimed the officials with whom I talked. "We holding King Nicholas a prisoner? The idea is preposterous. So far as France is concerned, he can return to Montenegro whenever he chooses."

Still, their protestations were not entirely convincing. Their attitude reminded me of the millionaire whose daughter, it was rumored, had eloped with the family chauffeur.

"Sure, she can marry him if she wants to," he told the reporters. "I have no objection. She is free, white, and twenty-one. But if she does marry him I'll stop her allowance, cut her out of my will, and never speak to her again."

Because it has been my privilege to know many sovereigns and because I have been honored with the confidence of several of them, I have become to a certain extent immune from the spell which seems to be exercised upon the commoner by personal contact with the Lord's anointed. Save when I have had some definite mission to accomplish, I have never had any overwhelming desire "to grasp the hand that shook the hand of John L. Sullivan." To me it seems an impertinence to take the time of busy men merely for the sake of being able to boast about it afterward to your friends. But because, during my travels in Jugoslavia, I heard King Nicholas repeatedly denounced by Serbian officials with far more bitterness than they employed toward their late enemies and oppressors, the Hapsburgs, I was frankly eager for an opportunity to form my own opinions about Montenegro's aged ruler. The opportunity came when, upon my return to Paris, I was informed that the King wished to meet me, he being desirous, I suppose, of talking with one who had come so recently from his own country.

At that time the King, with the Queen, Prince Peter, and his two unmarried daughters, was occupying a modest suite in the Hotel Meurice, in the rue de Rivoli. He received me in a large, sun-flooded room overlooking the Tuileries Gardens. The bald, broad-shouldered, rather bent old man in the blue serge suit, with a tin ear-trumpet in his hand, who rose from behind a great flat-topped desk to greet me, was a startling contrast to the tall and vigorous figure, in the picturesque dress of a Montenegrin chieftain, whom I had seen in Cetinje before the war. I looked at him with interest, for he has been on the throne longer than any living sovereign, he is the father-in-law of two Kings, and is connected by marriage with half the royal houses of Europe, and he is the last of that long line of patriarch-rulers who, leading their armies in person, have for more than two centuries maintained the independence of the Black Mountain and its people.

HIS MAJESTY NICHOLAS I. KING OF MONTENEGRO
He has been on the throne longer than any living sovereign, he is the father-in-law of two kings, and is connected by marriage with half the royal houses of Europe

The New Frontiers of Freedom: From the Alps to the Aegean

King Nicholas, as is generally known, has been remarkably successful in marrying off his daughters, two of them having married Kings, two others grand dukes, while a fifth became the wife of a Battenberg prince. Remembering this, I was sorely tempted to ask the King as to the truth of a story which I had heard in Cetinje years before. An English visitor to the Montenegrin capital had been invited to lunch at the palace. During the meal the King asked his guest his impressions of Montenegro.

"Its scenery is magnificent," was the answer. "Its women are as beautiful and its men as handsome as any I have ever seen. Their costumes are marvelously picturesque. But the country appears to have no exports, your Majesty."

"Ah, my friend," replied the King, his eyes twinkling, "you forget my daughters."

Another story, which illustrates the King's quick wit, was told me by his Majesty himself. When, some years before the Great War, Emperor Francis Joseph, on a yachting cruise down the Adriatic, dropped anchor in the Bocche di Cattaro, the Montenegrin mountaineers celebrated the imperial visit by lighting bonfires on their mountain peaks, a mile above the harbor.

"I see that you dwell in the clouds," remarked Francis Joseph to Nicholas, as they stood on the deck of the yacht after dinner watching the pin-points of flame twinkling high above them.

"Where else can I live?" responded the Montenegrin ruler. "Austria holds the sea; Turkey holds the land; the sky is all that is left for Montenegro."

One of the things which the King told me during our conversation will, I think, interest Americans. He said that when President Wilson arrived in Paris he sent him an autograph letter, congratulating him on the great part he had played in bringing peace to the world and requesting a personal interview.

"But he never granted me the interview," said the King sadly. "In fact, he never acknowledged my letter."

I attempted to bridge over the embarrassing pause by suggesting that perhaps the letter had never been received, but he waved aside the suggestion as unworthy of consideration. I gathered from what he said that royal letters do not miscarry.

"I realize that I am an old man and that my country is a very small and unimportant one," he continued, "while your President is the ruler of a great country and a very busy man. Still, we in Montenegro had heard so much of America's chivalrous attitude toward small, weak nations that I was unduly disappointed, perhaps, when my letter was ignored. I felt that my age, and the fact that I have occupied the throne of Montenegro for sixty years, entitled me to the consideration of a reply."

But we have strayed far from the road which we were traveling. Let us get back to the people of the mountains; I like them better than the politicians. Antivari, which nestles in a hollow of the hills, three or four miles inland from the port of the same name, is one of the most fascinating little towns in all the Balkans. Its narrow, winding, cobble-paved streets, shaded by canopies of grapevines and bordered by rows of squat, red-tiled houses, their plastered walls tinted pale blue, bright pink or yellow, and the amazingly picturesque costumes of its inhabitants—slender, stately Montenegrin women in long coats of turquoise-colored broad-cloth piped with crimson, Bosnians in skin-tight breeches covered with arabesques of braid and jackets heavy with embroidery, Albanians wearing the starched and pleated skirts of linen known as *fustanellas* and *comitadjis* with cartridge-filled bandoliers slung across their chests and their sashes bristling with assorted weapons, priests of the Orthodox Church with uncut hair and beards, wearing hats that look like inverted stovepipes, hook-nosed, white-bearded, patriarchal-looking Turks in flowing robes and snowy turbans, fierce-faced, keen-eyed mountain herdsmen in fur caps and coats of sheepskin—all these combined to make me feel that I had intruded upon the stage of a theater during a musical comedy performance, and that I must find the exit and escape before I was discovered by the stage-manager. If David Belasco ever visits Antivari he will probably try to buy the place bodily and transport it to East Forty-fourth Street and write a play around it.

The New Frontiers of Freedom: From the Alps to the Aegean

There were two gentlemen in Antivari whose actions gave me unalloyed delight. One of them, so I was told, was the head of the local anti-Serbian faction; the other, a human arsenal with weapons sprouting from his person like leaves from an artichoke, was the chief of a notorious band of *comitadjis*, as the Balkan guerrillas are called. They walked up and down the main street of Antivari, arms over each other's shoulders, heads close together, lost in conversation, but glancing quickly over their shoulders every now and then to see if they were in danger of being overheard, exactly like the plotters in a motion-picture play. From the earnestness of their conversation, the obvious awe in which they were held by the townspeople, and the suspicious looks cast in their direction by the Serbian gendarmes, I gathered that in the near future things were going to happen in that region. Approaching them, I haltingly explained, in the few words of Serbian at my command, that I was an American and that I wished to photograph them. Upon comprehending my request they debated the question for some moments, then shook their heads decisively. It was evident that, in view of what they had in mind, they considered it imprudent to have their pictures floating around as a possible means of identification. But while they were discussing the matter I took the liberty, without their knowledge, of photographing them anyway. It was as well, perhaps, that they did not see me do it, for the *comitadji* chieftain had a long knife, two revolvers, and four hand-grenades in his belt and a rifle slung over his shoulder.

From Antivari to Valona by sea is about as far as from New York to Albany by the Hudson, so that, leaving the Montenegrin port in the early morning, we had no difficulty in reaching the Albanian one before sunset. Before the war Valona—which, by the way, appears as Avlona on most American-made maps—was an insignificant fishing village, but upon Italy's occupation of Albania it became a military base of great importance. Whenever we had touched on our journey down the coast we had been warned against going to Valona because of the danger of contracting fever. The town stands on the edge of a marsh bordering the shore and, as no serious attempt has been made to drain the marsh or to clean up the town itself, about sixty per cent of the troops stationed there are constantly suffering from a peculiarly virulent form of malaria, similar to the Chagres fever of the Isthmus. The danger of contracting it was apparently considered very real, for, before we had been an hour in the quarters assigned to us, officers began to arrive with safeguards of one sort or another. One brought screens for all the windows; another provided mosquito-bars for the beds; a third presented us with disinfectant cubes, which we were to burn in our rooms several times each day; a fourth made us a gift of quinine pills, two of which we were to take hourly; still another of our hosts appeared with a dozen bottles of *acqua minerale* and warned us not to drink the local water, and, finally, to ensure us against molestation by prowling natives, a couple of sentries were posted beneath our windows.

"Valona isn't a particularly healthy place to live in, I gather?" I remarked, by way of making conversation, to the officer who was our host at dinner that evening. His face was as yellow as old parchment and he was shaking with fever.

"Well," he reluctantly admitted, "you must be careful not to be bitten by a mosquito or you will get malaria. And don't drink the water or you will contract typhoid. And keep away from the native quarter, for there is always more or less smallpox in the bazaars. And don't go wandering around the town after nightfall, for there's always a chance of some fanatic putting a knife between your shoulders. Otherwise, there isn't a healthier place in the world than Valona."

Across the street from the building in which we were quartered was a large mosque, which, judging from the scaffoldings around it, was under repair. But though it seemed to be a large and important mosque, there was no work going forward on it. I commented upon this one day to an officer with whom I was walking.

"Do you see those storks up there?" he asked, pointing to a pair of long-legged birds standing beside their nest on the dome of the mosque. "The stork is the sacred bird of Albania and if it makes its nest on a building which is in course of construction all work on that building ceases as long as the stork remains. A barracks we were erecting was held up for several months because a stork decided to make its nest in the rafters, whereupon the native workmen threw down their tools and quit."

The New Frontiers of Freedom: From the Alps to the Aegean

"In my country it is just the opposite," I observed. "There, when the stork comes, instead of stopping work they usually begin building a nursery."

TWO CONSPIRATORS OF ANTIVARI
They stood lost in conversation, heads close together, exactly like the plotters in a motion picture play

I had long wished to cross Albania and Macedonia, from the Adriatic to the Ægean, by motor, but the nearer we had drawn to Albania the more unlikely this project had seemed of realization. We were assured that there were no roads in the interior of the country or that such roads as existed were quite impassable for anything save ox-carts; that the country had been devastated by the fighting armies and that it would be impossible to get food en route; that the mountains we must cross were frequented by bandits and *comitadjis* and that we would be exposed to attack and capture; that, though the Italians might see us across Albania, the Serbian and Greek frontier guards would not permit us to enter Macedonia, and, as a final argument against the undertaking, we were warned that the whole country reeked with fever. But when I told the Governor-General of Albania, General Piacentini, what I wished to do every obstacle disappeared as though at the wave of a magician's wand.

"You will leave Valona early to-morrow morning," he said, after a short conference with his Chief of Staff. "You will be accompanied by an officer of my staff who was with the Serbian army on its retreat across Albania to the sea. The country is well garrisoned and I do not anticipate the slightest trouble, but, as a measure of precaution, a detachment of soldiers will follow your car in a motor-truck. You will spend the first night at Argirocastro, the second at Ljaskoviki, and the third at Koritza, which is occupied by the French. I will wire our diplomatic agent there to make arrangements with the Jugoslav authorities for you to cross the Serbian border to Monastir, where we still have a few troops engaged in salvage work. South of Monastir you will be in Greek territory, but I will wire the officer in command of the Italian forces at Salonika to take steps to facilitate your journey across Macedonia to the Ægean."

This journey across one of the most savage and least-known regions in all Europe was arranged as simply and matter-of-factly as a clerk in a tourist bureau would plan a motor trip through the White Mountains. With the exception of one or two alterations in the itinerary made necessary by tire trouble, the journey was made precisely as General Piacentini planned it and so complete were the arrangements we found that meals and sleeping quarters had been prepared for us in tiny mountain hamlets whose very names we had never so much as heard before.

Until its occupation by the Italians in 1917 Albania was not only the least-known region in Europe; it was one of the least-known regions in the world. Within sight of Italy, it was less known than many portions of Central Asia or Equatorial Africa. And it is still a savage country; a land but little changed since the days of Constantine and Diocletian; a land that for more than twenty centuries has acknowledged no master and, until the coming of the Italians, had known no law. Prior to the Italian occupation there was no government in Albania in the sense in which that word is generally used, there being, in fact, no civil government now, the tribal organization which takes its place being comparable to that which existed in Scotland under the Stuart Kings.

The term Albanian would probably pass unrecognized by the great majority of the inhabitants, who speak of themselves as *Skipétars* and of their country as *Sccupnj*. They are, most ethnologists agree, probably the most ancient race in Europe, there being every reason to believe that they are the lineal descendants of those adventurous Aryans who, leaving the ancestral home on the shores of the Caspian, crossed the Caucasus and entered Europe in the earliest dawn of history. One of the tribes of this migrating host, straying into these lonely valleys, settled there with their flocks and herds, living the same life, speaking the same tongue, following the same customs as their Aryan ancestors, quite indifferent to the great changes which were taking place in the world without their mountain wall. Certain it is that Albania was already an ancient nation when Greek history began. Unlike the other primitive populations of the Balkan peninsula, which became in time either Hellenized, Latinized or Slavonicized, the Albanians have remained almost unaffected by foreign influences. It strikes me as a strange thing that the courage and determination with which this remarkable race has maintained itself in its mountain stronghold all down the ages, and the grim and unyielding front which it has shown to innumerable invaders, have evoked so little appreciation and admiration in the outside world. History contains no such epic as that of the Albanian national hero, George Castriota, better known as Scanderbeg, who, with his ill-armed mountaineers, overwhelmed twenty-three Ottoman armies, one after another.

Picture, if you please, a country remarkably similar in its physical characteristics to the Blue Ridge Region of our own South, with the same warm summers and the same brief, cold winters, peopled by the same poverty-stricken, illiterate, quarrelsome, suspicious, arms-bearing, feud-practising race of mountaineers, and you will have the best domestic parallel of Albania that I can give you. Though during the summer months extremely hot days are followed by bitterly cold nights, and though fever is prevalent along the coast and in certain of the valleys, Albania is, climatically speaking, "a white man's country." Its mountains are believed to contain iron, coal, gold, lead, and copper, but the internal condition of the country has made it quite impossible to investigate its mineral resources, much less to develop them. With the exception of Valona, which has been developed into a tolerably good harbor, there are no ports worthy of the name, Durazzo, Santi Quaranta, and San Giovanni de Medua being mere open roadsteads, almost unprotected from the sea winds. There are no railroads in Albania, and the indifference of the Turkish Government, the corruption of the local chiefs, and the blood-feuds in which the people are almost constantly engaged, have resulted in a total absence of good roads. This condition has been remedied by the Italians, however, who, in order to facilitate their military operations, constructed a system of highways very nearly equal to those they built in the Alps. Though the greater part of the country is a stranger to the plow, the small areas which are under cultivation produce excellent olive oil, wine of a tolerable quality, a strong but moderately good tobacco, and considerable grain; Albania, in spite of its primitive agricultural methods, furnishing most of the corn supply of the Dalmatian coast.

Albania, so far as I am aware, is the only country where you can buy a wife on the instalment plan, just as you would buy a piano or an encyclopedia or a phonograph. It is quite true that there are plenty of countries where women can be purchased—in Circassia, for example, and in China, and in the Solomon Group—but in those places the prospective bridegroom is compelled to pay down the purchase price in cash, not being afforded the convenience of opening an account. In Albania, however, such things are better done, a partial payment on the purchase price of the girl being paid to her parents when the engagement takes place, after which she is no longer offered for sale, but is set aside, like an article on which a deposit has been made, until the final instalment has been paid, when she is delivered to her future husband.

THE HEAD MEN OF LJASKOVIKI, ALBANIA, WAITING TO BID MAJOR AND MRS. POWELL FAREWELL

Albania is likewise the only country that I know of where every one concerned becomes indignant if a murderer is sent to prison. The relatives of the dear departed resent it because they feel that the judge has cheated them out of their revenge, which they would probably obtain, were the murderer at large, by putting a knife or a pistol bullet between his shoulders. The murderer, of course, objects to the sentence both because he does not like imprisonment and because he believes that he could escape from the relatives of his victim were he given his freedom. If he or his friends have any money, however, the affair is usually settled on a financial basis, the feud is called off, the murderer is pardoned, and every one concerned, save only the dead man, is as pleased and friendly as though nothing had ever happened to interrupt their friendly relations. A quaint people, the Albanians.

In order to develop the resources of the country and to transform its present poverty into prosperity, Italy has already inaugurated an extensive scheme of public works, which includes the reclamation of the marshes, the reforestation of the mountains, the reconstruction of the highways, the improvement of the ports, and the construction of a railway straight across Albania, from the coast at Durazzo to Monastir, in Serbian Macedonia, where it will connect with the line from Belgrade to Salonika. This railway will follow the route of one of the most important arteries of the Roman Empire, the Via Egnatia, that mighty military and commercial highway, a trans-Adriatic continuation of the Via Appia, which, starting from Dyracchium, the modern Durazzo, crossed the Cavaia plain to the Skumbi, climbed the slopes of the Candavian range, and traversing Macedonia and Thrace, ended at the Bosphorus, thus linking the capitals of the western and the eastern empires. We traveled this age-old highway, down which the four-horse chariots of the Cæsars had rumbled two thousand years ago, in another sort of chariot, with the power of twenty times four horses beneath its sloping hood. This will entitle us in future years to listen with the condescension of pioneers to the tales of the tourists who make the same trans-Balkan journey in a comfortable *wagon-lit*, with hot and cold running water and electric lights and a dining-car ahead. It is a great thing to have seen a country in the pioneer stage of its existence.

In that portion of Southern Albania known as North Epirus we motored for an entire day through a region dotted with what had been, apparently, fairly prosperous towns and villages but which are now heaps of fire-blackened ruins. This wholesale devastation, I was informed to my astonishment, was the work of the Greeks, who, at about the time the Germans were horrifying the civilized world by their conduct in Belgium, were doing precisely the same thing, it is said, but on a far more extensive scale, in Albania. As a result of these atrocities, perpetrated by a so-called Christian and professedly civilized nation, a large number of Albanian towns and villages were destroyed by fire or dynamite. Though I have been unable to obtain any reliable figures, the consensus of opinion among the Albanians, the French and Italian officials, and the American missionaries and relief workers with whom I talked is that between 10,000 and 12,000 men, women, and children were shot, bayoneted, or burned to death, at least double that number died from exposure and starvation, and an enormous number—I have heard the figure placed as high as 200,000—were rendered homeless. The stories which I heard of the treatment to which the Albanian women were subjected are so revolting as to be unprintable. We spent a night at Ljaskoviki (also spelled Gliascovichi, Leskovik and Liascovik), three-quarters of which had been destroyed. Out of a population which, I was told, originally numbered about 8,000, only 1,200 remain.

Though the great majority of the victims were Mohammedans, the outrages were not directly due to religious causes but were inspired mainly by greed for territory. When, upon the erection of Albania into an independent kingdom in 1913, the Greeks were ordered by the Powers to withdraw from North Epirus, on which they had been steadily encroaching and which they had come to look upon as inalienably their own, they are reported to have begun a systematic series of outrages upon the civil population of the region for which a fitting parallel can be found only in the Turkish massacres in Armenia or the horrors of Bolshevik rule in Russia. In their determination to secure Southern Albania for themselves, the Greeks apparently adopted the policy followed with such success in Armenia by the Turks, who asserted cynically that "one cannot make a state without inhabitants."

I do not think that the Greeks attempt to deny these atrocities—the evidence is far too conclusive for that—but even as great a Greek as M. Venizelos justifies them on the ground that they were provoked by the Albanians. That such things could happen without arousing horror and condemnation throughout the civilized world is due to the fact that in the summer of 1914 the attention of the world was focused on events in France and Belgium. I have no quarrel with the Greeks and nothing is further from my desire than to engage in what used to be known as "muck-raking," but I am reporting what I saw and heard in Albania because I believe that the American people ought to know of it. Taken in conjunction with the behavior of the Greek troops in Smyrna in the spring of 1918, it should better enable us to form an opinion as to the moral fitness of the Greeks to be entrusted with mandates over backward peoples.

Though Albania is an Italian protectorate, the Albanians, in spite of all that Italy is doing toward the development of the country, do not want Italian protection. This is scarcely to be wondered at, however, in view of the attitude of another untutored people, the Egyptians, who, though they owe their amazing prosperity solely to British rule, would oust the British at the first opportunity which offered. Though the Italians are distrusted because the Albanians question their administrative ability and because they fear that they will attempt to denationalize them, the French are regarded with a hatred which I have seldom seen equaled. This is due, I imagine, to the belief that the French are allied with their hereditary enemies, the Greeks and the Serbs, and to France's iron-handed rule, which was exemplified when General Sarrail, commanding the army of the Orient, ordered the execution of the President of the short-lived Albanian Republic which was established at Koritza. As a matter of fact, the Albanians, though quite unfitted for independence, are violently opposed to being placed under the protection of any nation, unless it be the United States or England, in both of which they place implicit trust. I was astonished to learn that the few Americans who have penetrated Albania since the war—missionaries, Red Cross workers, and one or two investigators for the Peace Conference—have encouraged the natives in the belief that the United States would probably accept a mandate for Albania. Whether they did this in order to make themselves popular and thereby facilitate their missions, or because of an abysmal ignorance of American public sentiment, I do not know, but the fact remains that they have raised hopes in the breasts of thousands of Albanians which can never be realized. Everything considered, I think that the Albanians might do worse than to entrust their political future to the guidance of the Italians, who, in addition to having brought law, order, justice, and the beginnings of prosperity to a country which never had so much as a bowing acquaintance with any one of them before, seem to have the best interests of the people genuinely at heart.

Leaving Koritza, a clean, well-kept town of perhaps 10,000 people, which was occupied when we were there by a battalion of black troops from the French Sudan and some Moroccans, we went snorting up the Peristeri Range by an appallingly steep and narrow road, higher, higher, always higher, until, to paraphrase Kipling, we had

> "One wheel on the Horns o' the Mornin',
> An' one on the edge o' the Pit,
> An' a drop into nothin' beneath us
> As straight as a beggar could spit."

But at last, when I was beginning to wonder whether our wheels could find traction if the grade grew much steeper, we topped the summit of the pass and looked down on Macedonia. Below us the forested slopes of the mountains ran down, like the folds of a great green rug lying rumpled on an oaken floor, to meet the bare brown plains of that historic land where marched and fought the hosts of Philip of Macedon, and of Alexander, his son. There are few more splendid panoramas in the world; there is none over which history has cast so magic a spell, for this barren, dusty land has been the arena in which the races of eastern Europe have battled since history began. Within its borders are represented all the peoples who are disputing the reversion of the Turkish possessions in Europe. Macedonia might be described, indeed, as the very quintessence of the near eastern question.

With brakes a-squeal we slipped down the long, steep gradients to Florina, where Greek gendarmes, in British sun-helmets and khaki, lounged at the street-crossings and patronizingly waved us past. Thence north by the ancient highway which leads to Monastir, the parched and yellow fields on either side still littered with the débris of war—broken *camions* and wagons, shattered cannon, pyramids of ammunition-cases, vast quantities of barbed wire—and sprinkled with white crosses, thousands and thousands of them, marking the places where sleep the youths from Britain, France, Italy, Russia, Serbia, Canada, India, Australia, Africa, who fell in the Last Crusade.

Monastir is a filthy, ill-paved, characteristically Turkish town, which, before its decimation by the war, was credited with having some 60,000 inhabitants. Of these about one-half were Turks and one-quarter Greeks, the remaining quarter of the inhabitants being composed of Serbs, Jews, Albanians, and Bulgars. Those of its buildings which escaped the great conflagration which destroyed half the town were terribly shattered by the long series of bombardments, so that to-day the place looks like San Francisco after the earthquake and Baltimore after the fire. In the suburbs are immense supplies of war *matériel* of all sorts, mostly going to waste. I saw thousands of camions, ambulances, caissons, and wagons literally falling apart from neglect, and this in a country which is almost destitute of transport. Though the town was packed with Serbian troops, most of whom are sleeping and eating in the open, no attempt was being made, so far as I could see, to repair the shell-torn buildings, to clean the refuse-littered streets, or to afford the inhabitants even the most nominal police protection. The crack of rifles and revolvers is as frequent in the streets of Monastir as the bang of bursting tires on Fifth Avenue. A Serbian sentry, on duty outside the house in which I was sleeping, suddenly loosed off a clip of cartridges in the street, for no reason in the world, it seemed, than because he liked to hear the noise! Dead bodies are found nearly every morning. Murders are so common that they do not provoke even passing comment. In the night there comes a sharp bark of an automatic or the shattering roar of a hand-grenade (which, since the war proved its efficacy, has become the most recherché weapon for private use in these regions), a clatter of feet, and a "Hello! Another killing." That is all. Life is the cheapest thing there is in the Balkans.

The only really clean place we found in Monastir was the American Red Cross Hospital, an extremely well-managed and efficient institution, which was under the direction of a young American woman, Dr. Frances Flood, who,

with a single woman companion, Miss Jessup, pluckily remained at her post throughout the greater part of the war. The officers who during the war achieved rows of ribbons for having acted as messenger boys between the War Department and the foreign military missions in Washington, would feel a trifle embarrassed, I imagine, if they knew what this little American woman did to win *her* decorations.

The New Frontiers of Freedom: From the Alps to the Aegean

It is in the neighborhood of one hundred and fifty miles from Monastir to Salonika across the Macedonian plain and the road is one of the very worst in Europe. Deep ruts, into which the car sometimes slipped almost to its hubs, and frequent gullies made driving, save at the most moderate speed, impossible, while, as many of the bridges were broken, and without signs to warn the travelers of their condition, we more than once barely saved ourselves from plunging through the gaping openings to disaster. The vast traffic of the fighting armies had ground the roads into yellow dust which rose in clouds as dense as a London fog, while the waves of heat from the sun-scorched plains beat against our faces like the blast from an open furnace door. Despite its abominable condition, the road was alive with traffic: droves of buffalo, black, ungainly, broad-horned beasts, their elephant-like hides caked with yellow mud; woolly waves of sheep and goats driven by wild mountain herdsmen in high fur caps and gaudy sashes; caravans of camels, swinging superciliously past on padded feet, laden with supplies for the interior or salvaged war material for the coast; clumsy carts, painted in strange designs and screaming colors, with great sharpened stakes which looked as though they were intended for purposes of torture, but whose real duty is to keep the top-heavy loads in place.

Though the slopes of the Rhodope and the Pindus are clothed with splendid forests, it is for the most part a flat and treeless land, dotted with clusters of filthy hovels made of sun-dried brick and with patches of discouraged-looking vegetation. As Macedonia (its inhabitants pronounce it as though the first syllable were *mack*) was once the granary of the East, I had expected to see illimitable fields of waving grain, but such fields as we did see were generally small and poor. Guarding them against the hovering swarms of blackbirds were many scarecrows, rigged out in the uniforms and topped by the helmets of the men whose bones bleach amid the grain. In Switzerland they make a very excellent red wine called *Schweizerblut*, because the grapes from which it is made are grown on soil reddened by the blood of the Swiss who fell on the battlefield of Morat. If blood makes fine wine, then the best wine in all the world should come from these Macedonian plains, for they have been soaked with blood since ever time began.

The New Frontiers of Freedom: From the Alps to the Aegean

Our halfway town was Vodena, which seemed, after the heat and dust of the journey, like an oasis in the desert. Scores of streams, issuing from the steep slopes of the encircling hills, race through the town in a network of little canals and fling themselves from a cliff, in a series of superb cascades, into the wooded valley below. Philip of Macedon was born near Vodena, and there, in accordance with his wishes, he was buried. You can see the tomb, flanked by ever-burning candles, though you may not enter it, should you happen to pass that way. He chose his last resting-place well, did the great soldier, for the overarching boughs of ancient plane-trees turn the cobbled streets of the little town into leafy naves, the air is heavy with the scent of orange and oleander, and the place murmurs with the pleasant sound of plashing water.

Beyond Vodena the road improved for a time and we fled southward at greater speed, the telegraph poles leaping at us out of the yellow dust-haze like the pikes of giant sentinels. At Alexander's Well, an ancient cistern built from marble blocks and filled with crystal-clear water, we paused to refill our boiling radiator, and paused again, a few miles farther on, at the wretched, mud-walled village which, according to local tradition, is the birthplace of the man who made himself master of three continents, changed the face of the world, and died at thirty-three.

Then south again, south again, across the seemingly illimitable plains, until, topping a range of bare brown hills, there lay spread before us the gleaming walls and minarets of that city where Paul preached to the Thessalonians. To the westward Olympus seemed to verify the assertions of the ancient Greeks that its summit touched the sky. To the east, outlined against the Ægean's blue, I could see the peninsula of Chalkis, with its three gaunt capes, Cassandra, Longos, and Athos, reaching toward Thrace, the Hellespont and Asia Minor, like the claw of a vulture stretched out to snatch the quarry which the eagles killed.

CHAPTER IV

UNDER THE CROSS AND THE CRESCENT

Salonika is superbly situated. To gain it from the seaward side you sail through a portal formed by the majestic peaks of Athos and Olympus. It reclines on the bronze-brown Macedonian hills, white-clad, like a young Greek goddess, with its feet laved by the blue waters of the Ægean. (I have used this simile elsewhere in the book, but it does not matter.) The scores of slender minarets which rise above the housetops belie the crosses on the Greek flags which flaunt everywhere, hinting that the city, though it has passed under Christian rule, is at heart still Moslem. Indeed, barely a tenth of the 200,000 inhabitants are of the ruling race, for Salonika is that rare thing in modern Europe, a city whose population is by majority Jewish. There were hook-nosed, dark-skinned traders from Judea here, no doubt, as far back as the days when Salonika was but a way-station on the great highroad which linked the East with Rome, but it was the Jews expelled from Spain by Ferdinand and Isabella who transformed the straggling Turkish town into one of the most prosperous cities of the Levant by making it their home. And to-day the Jewish women of Salonika, the older ones at least, wear precisely the same costume that their great-grandmother wore in Spain before the persecution—a symbol and a reminder of how the Israelites were hunted by the Christians before they found refuge in a Moslem land.

There are no less than eight distinct ways of spelling and pronouncing the city's name. To the Greeks, who are its present owners, it is Saloniki or Saloneke, according to the method of transliterating the *epsilon*; it is known to the Turks, who misruled it for five hundred years, as Selanik; the British call it Salonica, with the accent on the second syllable; the French Salonique; the Italians Salonnico, while the Serbs refer to it as Solun. The best authorities seem to have agreed, however, on Salonika, with the accent on the "i," which is pronounced like "e," so that it rhymes with "paprika." But these are all corruptions and abbreviations, for the city was originally named Thessalonica, after the sister of Alexander of

The New Frontiers of Freedom: From the Alps to the Aegean

Macedon, and thus referred to in the two epistles which St. Paul addressed to the church he founded there. Owing to the variety of its religious sects, Salonika has a superfluity of Sabbaths as well as of names, Friday being observed by the Moslems, Saturday by the Jews, and Sunday by the Christians. Perhaps it would be putting it more accurately to say that there is no Sabbath at all, for the inhabitants are so eager to make money that business is transacted on every day of the seven.

THE ANCIENT WALLS OF SALONIKA
Before us we saw the yellow walls and crenellated towers of that city where Paul preached to the Thessalonians

Besides the great colony of Orthodox Jews in Salonika, there is a sect of renegades known as Dounmé, or Deunmeh, who number perhaps 20,000 in all. These had their beginnings in the *Annus Mirabilis*, when a Jewish Messiah, Sabatai Sevi of Smyrna, arose in the Levant. He preached a creed which was a first cousin of those believed in by our own Anabaptists and Seventh Day Adventists. The name and the fame of him spread across the Near East like fire in dry grass. Every ghetto in Turkey had accepted him; his ritual was adopted by every synagogue; the Jews gave themselves over to penance and preparation. For a year honesty reigned in the Levant. Then the prophet set out for Constantinople to beard the Sultan in his palace and, so he announced, to lead him in chains to Zion. That was where Sabatai Sevi made his big mistake. For the Commander of the

Faithful was from Missouri, so far as Sabatai Sevi's claims to divinity were concerned.

"Messiahs can perform miracles," the Sultan said. "Let me see you perform one. My Janissaries shall make a target of you. If you are of divine origin, as you claim, the arrows will not harm you. And, in any event, it will be an interesting experiment."

Now Sabatai evidently had grave doubts about his self-assumed divinity being arrow-proof, for he protested vigorously against the proposal to make a human pin-cushion of him, whereupon the Sultan, his suspicions now confirmed, gave him his choice between being impaled upon a stake, a popular Turkish pastime of the period, or of renouncing Judaism and accepting the faith of Islam. Preferring to be a live coward to an impaled martyr, he chose the latter, yet such was his influence with the Jews that thousands of his adherents voluntarily embraced the religion of Mohammed. The Dounmé of Salonika are the descendants of these renegades. Two centuries of waiting have not dimmed their faith in the eventual coming of their Messiah. So there they wait, equally distrusted by Jews and Moslems, though they form the wealthiest portion of the city's population. But they live apart and so dread any mixing of their blood with that of the infidel Turk or the unbelieving Jew that, in order to avoid the risk of an unwelcome proposal, they make a practise of betrothing their children before they are born. It strikes me, however, that there must on occasion be a certain amount of embarrasment connected with these early matches, as, for example, when the prenatally engaged ones prove to be of the same sex.

I used to be of the opinion that Tiflis, in the Caucasus, was the most cosmopolitan city that I had ever seen, but since the war I think that the greatest variety of races could probably be found in Salonika. Sit at a marble-topped table on the pavement in front of Floca's café at the tea-hour and you can see representatives of half the races in the world pass by—British officers in beautifully polished boots and beautifully cut breeches, astride of beautifully groomed ponies; Highlanders with their kilts covered by khaki aprons; raw-boned, red-faced Australians in sun helmets and shorts; swaggering *chausseurs d'Afrique* in wonderful uniforms of sky-blue and scarlet which you will find nowhere else outside a musical comedy; soldiers of the Foreign Legion with the skirts of their long blue overcoats pinned back and with mushroom-shaped helmets which are much too large for them; soldierly, well set-up little Ghurkas in broad-brimmed hats and uniforms of olive green, reminding one for all the world of fighting cocks; Sikhs in yellow khaki (did you know, by the way, that *khaki* is the Hindustani word for dust?) with their long black beards neatly plaited and rolled up under their chins; Epirotes wearing the starched and plaited skirts called *fustanellas*, each of which requires from twenty to forty yards of linen; Albanian tribal chiefs in jackets stiff with gold embroidery, with enough weapons thrust in their gaudy sashes to decorate a club-room; Cretan gendarmes wearing breeches which are so tight below the knee and so enormously baggy in the seat that they can, and when they are in Crete frequently do, use them in place of a basket for carrying their poultry, eggs or other farm produce to market; coal-black Senegalese, coffee-colored Moroccans and tan-colored Algerians, all wearing the broad red cummerbunds and the high red tarbooshes which distinguish France's African soldiery; Italian *bersaglieri* with great bunches of cocks' feathers hiding their steel helmets; Serbs in ununiform uniforms of every conceivable color, material and pattern, their only uniform article of equipment being their characteristic high-crowned *képis*; Russians in flat caps and belted blouses, their baggy trousers tucked into boots with ankles like accordions; officers of Cossack cavalry, their tall and slender figures accentuated by their long, tight-fitting coats and their high caps of lambskin; Bulgar prisoners wearing the red-banked caps which they have borrowed from their German allies and Austrian prisoners in worn and shabby uniforms of grayish-blue; Greek soldiers bedecked like Christmas trees with medals, badges, fourragéres and chevrons, in the hope, I suppose, that their gaudiness would make up for their lack of prowess; Orthodox priests with their long hair (for they never cut their hair or beards) done up in Psyche knots; Hebrew rabbis wearing caps of velvet shaped like those worn by bakers; Moslem muftis with their snowy turbans encircled by green scarves as a sign that they had made the pilgrimage to the Holy Places; Jewish merchants and money-changers in the same black caps and greasy gabardines which their ancestors wore in the Middle Ages; British,

French, Italian and American bluejackets with their caps cocked jauntily and the roll of the sea in their gait; A.R.A., A.R.C., Y.M.C.A., K. of C. and A.C.R.N.E. workers in fancy uniforms of every cut and color; Turkish sherbet-sellers with huge brass urns, hung with tinkling bells to give notice of their approach, slung upon their backs; ragged Macedonian bootblacks (bootblacking appeared to be the national industry of Macedonia), and hordes of gipsy beggars, the filthiest and most importunate I have ever seen. All day long this motley, colorful crowd surges through the narrow streets, their voices, speaking in a score of tongues, raising a din like that of Bedlam; the smells of unwashed bodies, human perspiration, strong tobacco, rum, hashish, whiskey, arrack, goat's cheese, garlic, cheap perfumery and sweat-soaked leather combining in a stench which rises to high Heaven.

On the streets one sees almost as many colored soldiers as white ones: French native troops from Algeria, Morocco, Madagascar, Senegal and China; British Indian soldiery from Bengal, the Northwest Provinces and Nepaul. The Indian troops were superbly drilled and under the most iron discipline, but the French native troops appeared to be getting out of hand and were not to be depended upon. To a man they had announced that they wanted to go home. They had been through four and a half years of war, they are tired and homesick, and they are more than willing to let the Balkan peoples settle their own quarrels. They were weary of fighting in a quarrel of which they knew little and about which they cared less; they longed for a sight of the wives and the children they had left behind them in Fez or Touggourt or Timbuktu. Because they had been kept on duty in Europe, while the French white troops were being rapidly demobilized and returned to their homes, the Africans were sullen and resentful. This smoldering resentment suddenly burst into flame, a day or so before we reached Salonika, when a Senegalese sergeant, whose request to be sent home had been refused, ran amuck, barricaded himself in a stone outhouse with a plentiful supply of rifles and ammunition, and succeeded in killing four officers and half-a-dozen soldiers before his career was ended by a well-aimed hand grenade. A few days later a British officer was shot and killed in the camp outside the city by a Ghurka sentinel. This was not due to mutiny, however, but, on the contrary, to over-strict obedience to orders, the sentry having been instructed that he was to permit no one to cross his post without challenging. The officer, who was fresh from England and had had no experience with the discipline of Indian troops, ignored the order to halt—and the next day there was a military funeral.

Salonika is theoretically under Greek rule and there are pompous, self-important little Greek policemen, perfect replicas of the British M.P.'s in everything save physique and discipline, on duty at the street crossings, but instead of regulating the enormous flow of traffic they seem only to obstruct it. When the congestion becomes so great that it threatens to hold up the unending stream of motor-lorries which rolls through the city, day and night, between the great cantonments in the outskirts and the port, a tall British military policeman suddenly appears from nowhere, shoulders the Greek gendarme aside, and with a few curt orders untangles the snarl into which the traffic has gotten itself and sets it going again.

Picturesque though Salonika undeniably is, with its splendid mosques, its beautiful Byzantine churches, its Roman triumphal arches, and the brooding bulk of Mount Olympus, which overshadows and makes trivial everything else, yet the strongest impressions one carries away are filth, corruption and misgovernment. These conditions are due in some measure, no doubt, to the refusal of the European troops, with whom the city is filled, to take orders from any save their own officers, but the underlying reason is to be found in the indifference and gross incompetence of the Greek authorities. The Greeks answer this by saying that they have not had time to clean the city up and give it a decent administration because they have owned it only eight years. All of the European business quarter, including a mile of handsome buildings along the waterfront, lies in ruins as a result of the great fire of 1917. Though a system of new streets has been tentatively laid out across this fire-swept area, no attempt has been made to rebuild the city, hundreds of shopkeepers carrying on their businesses in shacks and booths erected amid the blackened and tottering walls. All of the hotels worthy of the name were destroyed in the fire, the two or three which escaped being quite uninhabitable, at least for Europeans, because of the armies of insects with which they are infested. I do not recall hearing any one say a good word for Salonika. The pleasantest recollection which I retain of the place is that of the steamer which took us away from there.

Before we could leave Salonika for Constantinople our passports had to be viséd by the representatives of five nations. In fact, travel in the Balkans since the war is just one damn visé after another. The Italians stamped them because we had come from Albania, which is under Italian protection. The Serbs put on their imprint because we had stopped for a few days in Monastir. The Greeks affixed their stamp—and collected handsomely for doing so—because, theoretically at least, Salonika, whose dust we were shaking from our feet, belongs to them. The French insisted on viséing our papers in order to show their authority and because they needed the ten francs. The British control officer told me that I really didn't need his visé, but that he would put it on anyway because it would make the passports look more imposing. Because we were going to Constantinople and Bucharest, whereas our passports were made out for "the Balkan States," the American Consul would not visé them at all, on the ground that neither Turkey nor Roumania is in the Balkans. About Roumania he was technically correct, but I think most geographers place European Turkey in the Balkans. As things turned out, however, it was all labor lost and time thrown away, for we landed in Constantinople as untroubled by officials and inspectors as though we were stepping ashore at Twenty-third Street from a Jersey City ferry.

There were no regular sailings from Salonika for Constantinople, but, by paying a hundred dollars for a ticket which in pre-war days cost twenty, we succeeded in obtaining passage on an Italian tramp steamer. The *Padova* was just such a cargo tub as one might expect to find plying between Levantine ports. Though we occupied an officer's cabin, for which we were charged *Mauretania* rates, it was very far from being as luxurious as it sounds, for I slept upon a mattress laid upon three chairs and the mattress was soiled and inhabited. Still, it was very diverting, after an itching night, to watch the cockroaches, which were almost as large as mice, hurrying about their duties on the floor and ceiling. Huddled under the forward awnings were two-score deck passengers—Greeks, Turks,

Armenians and Roumanians. Sprawled on their straw-filled mattresses, they loafed the hot and lazy days away in playing cards, eating the black bread, olives and garlic which they had brought with them, smoking a peculiarly strong and villainous tobacco, and torturing native musical instruments of various kinds. At night a young Turk sang plaintive, quavering laments to the accompaniment of a sort of guitar, some of the others occasionally joining in the mournful chorus. I found my chief recreation, when it grew too dark to read, in watching an Orthodox priest, who was one of the deck-passengers, prepare for the night by combing and putting up his long and greasy hair. Another of the deck-passengers was a rather prosperous-looking, middle-aged Levantine who had been in America making his fortune, he told me, and was now returning to his wife, who lived in a little village on the Dardanelles, after an absence of sixteen years. She had no idea that he was coming, he said, as he had planned to surprise her. Perhaps he was the one to be surprised. Sixteen years is a long time for a woman to wait for a man, even in a country as conservative as Turkey.

The officers of the *Padova* talked a good deal about the mine-fields that still guarded the approaches to the Dardanelles and the possibility that some of the deadly contrivances might have broken loose and drifted across our course. In order to cheer us up the captain showed us the charts, on which the mined areas were indicated by diagonal shadings, little red arrows pointing the way between them along channels as narrow and devious as a forest trail. To add to our sense of security he told us that he had never been through the Dardanelles before, adding that he did not intend to pick up a pilot, as he considered their charges exorbitant. At the base of the great mine-field which lies across the mouth of the Straits we were hailed by a British patrol boat, whose choleric commander bellowed instructions at us, interlarded with much profanity, through a megaphone. The captain of the *Padova* could understand a few simple English phrases, if slowly spoken, but the broadside of Billingsgate only confused and puzzled him, so, despite the fact that he had no pilot and that darkness was rapidly descending, he kept serenely on his course. This seemed to enrage the British skipper, who threw over his wheel and ran directly across our bows, very much as one polo player tries to ride off another.

"You — — fool!" he bellowed, fairly dancing about his quarter-deck with rage. "Why in hell don't you stop when I tell you to? Don't you know that you're running straight into a mine-field? Drop anchor alongside me and do it — — quick or I'll take your — — license away from you. And I don't want any of your — — excuses, either. I won't listen to 'em."

"What he say?" the captain asked me. "I not onderstan' hees Engleesh ver' good."

"No, you wouldn't," I told him. "He's speaking a sort of patois, you see. He wants to know if you will have the great kindness to drop anchor alongside him until morning, for it is forbidden to pass through the mine-fields in the dark, and he hopes that you will have a very pleasant night."

Five minutes later our anchor had rumbled down off Sed-ul-Bahr, under the shadow of Cape Helles, the tip of that rock, sun-scorched, blood-soaked peninsula which was the scene of that most heroic of military failures—the Gallipoli campaign. Above us, on the bare brown hillside, was what looked, in the rapidly deepening twilight, like a patch of driven snow, but upon examining it through my glasses I saw that it was a field enclosed by a rude wall and planted thickly with small white wooden crosses, standing row on row. Then I remembered. It was at the foot of these steep and steel-swept bluffs that the Anzacs made their immortal landing; it is here, in earth soaked with their own blood, that they lie sleeping. The crowded dugouts in which they dwelt have already fallen in; the trenches which they dug and which they held to the death have crumbled into furrows; their bones lie among the rocks and bushes at the foot of that dark and ominous hill on whose slopes they made their supreme sacrifice. Leaning on the rail of the deserted bridge in the darkness and the silence it seemed as though I could see their ghosts standing amid the crosses on the hillside staring longingly across the world toward that sun-baked Karroo of Australia and to the blue New Zealand mountains which they called "Home." It was a night never to be forgotten, for the glassy surface of the Ægean glowed with phosphorescence, the sky was like a hanging of purple velvet, and the peak of our foremast seemed almost to graze the stars.

Across the Hellespont, to the southward, the sky was illumined by a ruddy glow—a village burning, so a sailor told me, on the site of ancient Troy. And then there came back to me those lines from Agamemnon which I had learned as a boy:

"Beside the ruins of Troy they lie buried, those men so beautiful; there they have their burial-place, hidden in an enemy's land!"

We got under way at daybreak and, picking our way as cautiously as a small boy who is trying to get out of the house at night without awakening his family, we crept warily through the vast mine-field which was laid across the entrance to the Dardanelles, past Sed-ul-Bahr, whose sandy beach is littered with the rusting skeletons of both Allied and Turkish warships and transports; past Kalid Bahr, where the high bluffs are dotted with the ruins of Turkish forts destroyed by the shell-fire of the British dreadnaughts on the other side of the peninsula and with the remains of other forts which were destroyed in the Crusaders' times; past Chanak, where the steep hill-slopes behind the town were white with British tents, and so into the safe waters of the Marmora Sea. Though I was perfectly familiar with the topography of the Gallipoli Peninsula, as well as with the possibilities of modern naval guns, I was astonished at the evidences, which we saw along the shore for miles, of the extraordinary accuracy of the fire of the British fleet. Virtually all the forts defending the Dardanelles were bombarded by indirect fire, remember, the whole width of the peninsula separating them from the fleet. To get a mental picture of the situation you must imagine warships lying in the East River firing over Manhattan Island in an attempt to reduce fortifications on the Hudson. Men who were in the Gallipoli forts during the bombardment told me that, though they were prevented by the rocky ridge which forms the spine of the peninsula from seeing the British warships, and though, for the same reason, the gunners on the ships could not see the forts, the great steel calling-cards of the British Empire came falling out of nowhere as regularly and with as deadly precision as though they were being fired at point-blank range.

The successful defense of the Dardanelles, one of the most brilliantly conducted defensive operations of the entire war, was primarily due to the courage and stubborn endurance of Turkey's Anatolian soldiery, ignorant, stolid, hardy, fearless peasants, who were taken straight from their farms in Asia Minor, put into wretchedly made, ill-fitting uniforms, hastily trained by German drillmasters, set down in the trenches on the Gallipoli ridge and told to hold them. No one who is familiar with the conditions under which these Turkish soldiers fought, who knows how wretched were the conditions under which they lived, who has seen those waterless, sun-seared ridges which they held against the might of Britain's navy and the best troops which the Allies could bring against them, can withhold from them his admiration. Their valor was deserving of a better cause.

CHAPTER V

WILL THE SICK MAN OF EUROPE RECOVER?

Each time that I have approached Constantinople from the Marmora Sea and have watched that glorious and fascinating panorama—Seraglio Point, St. Sophia, Stamboul, the Golden Horn, the Galata Bridge, the heights of Pera, Dolmabagtche, Yildiz—slowly unfold, revealing new beauties, new mysteries, with each revolution of the steamer's screw, I have declared that in all the world there is no city so lovely as this capital of the Caliphs. Yet, beautiful though Constantinople is, it combines the moral squalor of Southern Europe with the physical squalor of the Orient to a greater degree than any city in the Levant. Though it has assumed the outward appearance of a well-organized and fairly well administered municipality since its occupation by the Allies, one has but to scratch this thin veneer to discover that the filth and vice and corruption and misgovernment which characterized it under Ottoman rule still remain. Barring a few municipal improvements which were made in the European quarter of Pera and in the fashionable residential districts between Dolmabagtche and Yildiz, the Turkish capital has scarcely a bowing acquaintance with modern sanitation, the windows of some of the finest residences in Stamboul looking out on open sewers down which refuse of every description floats slowly to the sea or takes lodgment on the banks, these masses of decaying matter attracting great swarms of pestilence-breeding flies. The streets are thronged with women whose virtue is as easy as an old shoe, attracted by the presence of the armies as vultures are attracted by the smell of carrion. Saloons, brothels, dives and gambling hells run wide open and virtually unrestricted, and as a consequence venereal diseases abound, though the British military authorities, in order to protect their own men, have put the more notorious resorts "out of bounds" and, in order to provide more wholesome recreations for the troops, have opened amusement parks called "military gardens." In spite of the British, French, Italian and Turkish military police who are on duty in the streets, stabbing affrays, shootings and robberies are so common that they provoke but little comment. Petty thievery is universal. Hats, coats, canes, umbrellas disappear from beside one's chair in hotels and restaurants. The Pera Palace Hotel has notices posted in its corridors warning the guests that it is no longer safe to place their shoes outside their doors to be polished. The streets, always wretchedly paved, have been ground to pieces by the unending procession of motor-lorries, and, as they are never by any chance repaired, the first rain transforms them into a series of hog-wallows. The most populous districts of Pera, of Galata, and of Stamboul are now disfigured by great areas of fire-blackened ruins—reminders of the several terrible conflagrations from which the Turkish capital has suffered in recent years. "Should the United States decide to accept the mandate for Constantinople," a resident remarked to me, "these burned districts would give her an opportunity to start rebuilding the city on modern sanitary lines" and, he might have added, at American expense.

The prices of necessities are fantastic and of luxuries fabulous. The cost of everything has advanced from 200 to 1,200 per cent. The price of a meal is no longer reckoned in piastres but in Turkish pounds, though this is not as startling as it sounds, for the Turkish *lira* has dropped to about a quarter of its normal value. Quite a modest dinner for two at such places as Tokatlian's, the Pera Palace Hotel, or the Pera Gardens, costs the equivalent of from fifteen to twenty dollars. Everything else is in proportion. From the "Little Club" in Pera to the Galata Bridge is about a seven minutes' drive by carriage. In the old days the standard tariff for the trip was twenty-five cents. Now the cabmen refuse to turn a wheel for less than two dollars.

Speaking of money, the chief occupation of the traveler in the Balkans is exchanging the currency of one country for that of another: lira into dinars, dinars into drachmæ, drachmæ into piastres, piastres into leva, leva into lei, lei into roubles (though no one ever exchanges his money for roubles if he can possibly help it), roubles into kronen, and kronen into lire again. The idea is to leave each country with as little as possible of that country's currency in your possession. It is like playing that card game in which you are penalized for every heart you have left in your hand.

The New Frontiers of Freedom: From the Alps to the Aegean

"But how is the Sick Man?" I hear you ask.

He is doing very nicely, thank you. In fact, he appears to be steadily improving. There was a time, shortly after the Armistice, when it seemed certain that he would have to submit to an operation, which he probably would not have survived, but the surgeons disagreed as to the method of operating and now it looks as though he would get well in spite of them. He has a chill every time they hold a consultation, of course, but he will probably escape the operation altogether, though he may have to take some extremely unpleasant medicine and be kept on a diet for several years to come. He has remarkable recuperative powers, you know, and his friends expect to see him up and about before long.

That may sound flippant, as it is, but it sums up in a single paragraph the extraordinary political situation which exists in Turkey to-day. Little more than a year ago Turkey surrendered in defeat, her resources exhausted, her armies destroyed or scattered. If anything in the world seemed certain at that time it was that the redhanded nation, whose very name has for centuries been a synonym for cruelty and oppression, would disappear from the map of Europe, if not from the map of the world, at the behest of an outraged civilization. The Turkish Government committed the most outrageous crime of the entire war when it organized the systematic extermination of the Armenians. Its former Minister of War, Enver Pasha, has been quoted as cynically remarking, "If there are no more Armenians there can be no Armenian question." A people capable of such barbarity ought no longer be permitted to sully Europe with their presence: they ought to be driven back into those savage Anatolian regions whence they came and kept there, just as those suffering from a less objectionable form of leprosy are confined on Molokai. But the fervor of a year ago for expelling the Turks from Europe is rapidly dying down. In the spring of 1919 Turkey could have been partitioned by the Allies with comparatively little friction. No one expected it more than Turkey herself. Whenever she heard a step on the floor, a knock at the door, she keyed herself for the ordeal of the anesthetic and the operating table. But the ancient jealousies and rivalries of the Entente nations, which had been forgotten during the war, returned with peace and now it looks as though, as a result of these nations' distrust and suspicion of each other, the Turks would win back by diplomacy what they lost in battle. How History repeats itself! The Turks have often been unlucky in war and then had a return of luck at the peace table. It was so after the Russo-Turkish War, when the Congress of Berlin tore up the Treaty of San Stefano. It was so to a lesser extent after the Balkan wars, when the interference of the European Concert enabled Turkey to recover Adrianople and a portion of the Thracian territory which she had lost to Bulgaria. And now it looks as though she were once again to escape the punishment she so richly merits. If she does, then History will chronicle few more shameful miscarriages of justice.

If the people of the United States could know for a surety of the avarice, the selfishness, the cynicism which have marked every step of the negotiations relative to the settlement of the Near Eastern Question, if they were aware of the chicanery and the deceit and the low cunning practised by the European diplomatists, I am convinced that there would be an irresistible demand that we withdraw instantly from participation in the affairs of Southeastern Europe and of Western Asia. Why not look the facts in the face? Why not admit that these affairs are, after all, none of our concern, and that, by every one save the Turks and the Armenians, our attempted dictation is resented. In the language of the frontier, we have butted into a game in which we are not wanted. It is no game for up-lifters or amateurs. England, France, Italy and Greece are not in this game to bring order out of chaos but to establish "spheres of influence." They are not thinking about self-determination and the rights of little peoples and making the world safe for Democracy; they are thinking in terms of future commercial and territorial advantage. They are playing for the richest stakes in the history of the world: for the control of the Bosphorus and the Bagdad Railway—for whoever controls them controls the trade routes to India, Persia, and the vast, untouched regions of Transcaspia; the commercial domination of Western Asia, and the overlordship of that city which stands at the crossroads of the Eastern World and its political capital of Islam.

In order better to appreciate the subtleties of the game which they are playing, let us glance over the shoulders of the players, and get a glimpse of their hands. Take England to begin with. Unless I am greatly mistaken, England is not in favor of a complete dismemberment of Turkey or the expulsion of the Sultan from Constantinople. This is a complete *volte face* from the sentiment in England immediately after the war, but during the interim she has heard in no uncertain terms from her 100,000,000 Mohammedan subjects in India, who look on the Turkish Sultan as the head of their religion and who would resent his humiliation as deeply, and probably much more violently, than the Roman Catholics would resent the humiliation of the Pope. British rule in India, as those who are in touch with Oriental affairs know, is none too stable, and the last thing in the world England wants to do is to arouse the hostility of her Moslem subjects by affronting the head of their faith. England will unquestionably retain control of Mesopotamia for the sake of the oil wells at the head of the Persian Gulf, the control which it gives her of the eastern section of the Bagdad Railway, and because of her belief that scientific irrigation will once more transform the plains of Babylonia into one of the greatest wheat-producing regions in the world. She may, and probably will, keep her oft-repeated promises to the Jews by erecting Palestine into a Hebrew kingdom under British protection, if for no other reason than its value as a buffer state to protect Egypt. She will also, I assume, continue to foster and support the policy of Pan-Arabism, as expressed In the new Kingdom of the Hedjaz, not alone for the reason that control of the Arabian peninsula gives her complete command of the Red Sea and the Persian Gulf as well as a highroad from Egypt to her new protectorate of Persia, but because she hopes, I imagine, that her protege, the King of Hedjaz, as Sheriff of Mecca, will eventually supplant the Sultan as the religious head of Islam. (It is interesting to note, in passing, that, as a result of the protectorates which she has proclaimed over Mesopotamia, Palestine, Arabia and Persia, England has, as a direct result of the war, obtained control of new territories in Asia alone having an area greater than that of all the states east of the Mississippi put together, with a population of some 20,000,000.) Though England would unquestionably welcome the United States accepting a mandate for Constantinople, which would ensure the neutrality of the Bosphorus, and for Armenia, which, under American protection, would form a stabilized buffer state on Mesopotamia's northern border, I am convinced that, even if the

The New Frontiers of Freedom: From the Alps to the Aegean

United States refuses such mandates, the British Government will oppose the serious humiliation of the Sultan-Khalif, or the complete dismemberment of his dominions.

The latest French plan is to establish an independent Turkey from Adrianople to the Taurus Mountains, lopping off Syria, which will become a French protectorate, and Mesopotamia and Palestine, which will remain under British control.

Constantinople, according to the French view, must remain independent, though doubtless the freedom of the Straits would be assured by some form of international control. France is not particularly enthusiastic about the establishment of an independent Armenia, for many French politicians believe that the interests of the Armenians can be safeguarded while permitting them to remain under the nominal suzerainty of Turkey, but she will oppose no active objections to Armenian independence. But there must be no crusade against the Turkish Nationalists who are operating in Asia Minor and no pretext given for Nationalist massacres of Greeks and Armenians. And the Sultan must retain the Khalifate and his capital in Constantinople, for, according to the French view, it is far better for the interests of France, who has nearly 30,000,000 Moslem subjects of her own, to have an independent head of Islam at Constantinople, where he would be to a certain extent under French influence, than to have a British-controlled one at Mecca. The truth of the matter is that France is desperately anxious to protect her financial interests in Turkey, which are already enormous, and she knows perfectly well that her commercial and financial ascendency on the Bosphorus will suddenly wane if the Empire should be dismembered. That is the real reason why she is cuddling up to the Sick Man. Being perfectly aware that neither England nor Italy would consent to her becoming the mandatary for Constantinople, she proposes to do the next best thing and rule Turkey in the future, as in the past, through the medium of her financial interests. Sophisticated men who have read the remarkable tributes to Turkey which have been appearing in the French press, and its palliation of her long list of crimes, have been aware that something was afoot, but only those who have been on the inside of recent events realize how enormous are the stakes, and how shrewd and subtle a game France is playing.

Strictly speaking, Italy is not one of the claimants to Constantinople. Not that she does not want it, mind you, but because she knows that there is about as much chance of her being awarded such a mandate as there is of her obtaining French Savoy, which she likewise covets. Under no conceivable conditions would France consent to the Bosphorus passing under Italian control; according to French views, indeed, Italy is already far too powerful in the Balkans. Recognizing the hopelessness of attempting to overcome French opposition, Italy has confined her claims to the great rich region of Cilicia, which roughly corresponds to the Turkish vilayet of Adana, a rich and fertile region in southern Asia Minor, with a coast line stretching from Adana to Alexandretta. Cilicia, I might mention parenthetically, is usually included in the proposed Armenian state, and Armenians have anticipated that Alexandretta would be their port on the Mediterranean, but, while the peacemakers at Paris have been discussing the question, Italy has been pouring her troops into this region, having already occupied the hinterland as far back as Konia. Italy's sole claim to this region is that she wants it and that she is going to take it while the taking is good. There are, it is true, a few Italians along the coast, there are some Italian banks, and considerable Italian money has been invested in various local projects, but the population is overwhelmingly Turkish. But, as the Italians point out in defending this piece of land-grabbing, Article 22 of the Covenant of the League of Nations expressly states that the wishes of people not yet civilized need not be considered.

Let us now consider the claims of Greece as a reversionary of the Sick Man's estate. Considering their attitude during the early part of the war (for it is no secret that General Sarrail's operations in Macedonia were seriously hampered by his fear that Greece might attack him in the rear) and the paucity of their losses in battle, the Greeks have done reasonably well in the game of territory grabbing. Do you realize, I wonder, the full extent of the Hellenic claims? Greece asks for (1) the southern portion of Albania, known as North Epirus; (2) for the whole of Bulgarian Thrace, thus completely barring Bulgaria from the Ægean; (3) for the whole of European

Turkey, including the Dardanelles and Constantinople; (4) for the province of Trebizond, on the southern shore of the Black Sea, the Greek inhabitants of which attempted to establish the so-called Pontus Republic; (5) the great seaport of Smyrna, with its 400,000 inhabitants, and a considerable portion of the hinterland, which she has already occupied; (6) the Dodecannessus Islands, of which the largest is Rhodes, off the western coast of Asia Minor, which the Italians occupied during the Turco-Italian War and which they have not evacuated; (7) the cession of Cyprus by England, which has administered it since 1878. Greece's modest demands might be summed up in the words of a song which was popular in the United States a dozen years ago and which might appropriately be adopted by the Greeks as their national anthem:

> "All I want is fifty million dollars,
> A champagne fountain flowing at my feet;
> J. Pierpont Morgan waiting at the table,
> And Sousa's band a-playing while I eat."

I will be quite candid in saying that I have small sympathy for Greece's claims to these territories, not because she is not entitled to them on the ground of nationality—for there is no denying that, in all of the regions in question, save only Albania and Thrace, Greeks form a majority of the Christian inhabitants—but because she is not herself sufficiently advanced to be entrusted with authority over other races, particularly over Mohammedans. The atrocities committed by Greek troops on the Moslems of Albania and of Smyrna, to say nothing of the behavior of the Greek bands in Macedonia during the Balkan wars, should be sufficient proof of her unfitness to govern an alien race. I have already spoken in some detail of the reported Greek outrages in Albania. But this was not an isolated instance of the methods employed in "Hellenizing" Moslem populations. In the spring of 1919 the Peace Conference, hypnotized, apparently, by M. Venizelos, who is one of the ablest diplomats of the day, made the mistake of permitting Greek forces, unaccompanied by other troops, to land at Smyrna. Almost immediately there began an indiscriminate slaughter of Turkish officials and civilians, in retaliation, so the Greeks assert, for the massacre of Greeks by Turks in the outlying districts. The obvious answer to this is that, while the Greeks claim that they are a civilized race, they assert that the Turks are not. The outcry against the Greeks on this occasion was so great that an inter-allied commission, including American representatives, was appointed to make a thorough investigation. This commission unanimously found the Greeks guilty of the unprovoked massacre of 800 Turkish men, women and children, who were shot down in cold blood while being marched along the Smyrna waterfront, those who were not killed instantly being thrown by Greek soldiers into the sea. High handed and outrageous conduct by Greek troops in the towns and villages back of Smyrna was also proved. I do not require any further testimony as to the unwisdom of placing Mohammedans under Greek control, but, if I did, I have the evidence of Mr. Hamlin, the son of the founder of Roberts College, who was born in the Levant, who speaks both Turkish and Greek, and who was sent to Smyrna by the Greek government as an investigator and adviser. He told me that the Greek attitude toward the Moslems was highly provocative and overbearing and that the Allies were guilty of criminal negligence when they permitted the Greeks to land at Smyrna alone.

Though they know that their dream of restoring Hellenic rule over Byzantium cannot be realized, the Greeks are bitterly opposed to the United States receiving a mandate for Constantinople. The extent of Greek hostility toward the United States is not appreciated in America, yet I found traces of it everywhere in the Levant. A widespread Greek propaganda has laid the responsibility for Greece's failure to get the whole of Thrace at the door of the United States. To this accusation has been added the charge that Americans were foremost in creating sentiment against the Greek massacres in Smyrna, which, the Greeks contend, was merely an unfortunate incident and should be overlooked. All sorts of extraordinary reasons are advanced for America's alleged hostility to Greek claims, ranging from the charge that our attitude is inspired by the missionaries (for the Orthodox Church has always opposed the presence of American missionaries in Greek lands) to commercial ambition. As one leading Greek paper put it, "Alongside of America's greed and schemes for commercial expansion since the war, Germany's imperialism was pure idealism."

The New Frontiers of Freedom: From the Alps to the Aegean

YILDIZ KIOSK, THE FAVORITE PALACE OF ABDUL-HAMID AND HIS SUCCESSORS ON THE THRONE OF OSMAN
The building in the foreground, known as the Ambassador's Pavilion, is only a small portion of the great Palace which in Abdul-Hamid's time housed upward of 10,000 persons

And now a few words as to the attitude of Turkey herself, for she has, after all, a certain interest in the matter. The Turks are perfectly resigned to accepting either America, England or France as mandatary, though they would much prefer America, provided that European Turkey, Anatolia and Armenia are kept together, for they realize that Syria, Mesopotamia and Arabia, whose populations are overwhelmingly Arab, are lost to them forever. What they would most eagerly welcome would be an American mandate for European Turkey and the whole of Asia Minor, including Armenia. This would keep out the Greeks, whom they hate, and the Italians, whom they distrust, and it would keep intact the most valuable portion of the Empire and the part for which they have the deepest sentimental attachment. Most Turks believe that, with America as the mandatary power, the country would not only benefit enormously through the railways, roads, harbor works, agricultural projects, sanitary improvements and financial reforms which would be carried out at American expense, as in the Philippines, but that, should the Turks behave themselves and demonstrate an ability for self-government, America would eventually restore their complete independence, as she has promised to restore that of the Filipinos. But if they find that

Constantinople and Armenia are to be taken away from them, then I imagine that they would vigorously oppose any mandatary whatsoever. And they could make a far more effective opposition than is generally believed, for, though Constantinople is admittedly at the mercy of the Allied fleet in the Bosphorus, the Nationalist are said to have recruited a force numbering nearly 300,000 men, composed of well-trained and moderately well equipped veterans of the Gallipoli campaign, which is concentrated in the almost inaccessible regions of Central Anatolia. Moreover, Enver Pasha, the former Minister of War and leader of the Young Turk party, who, it is reported, has made himself King of Kurdistan, is said to be in command of a considerable force of Turks, Kurds and Georgians which he has raised for the avowed purpose of ending the troublesome Armenian question by exterminating what is left of the Armenians, and by effecting a union of the Turks, the Kurds, the Mohammedans of the Caucasus, the Persians, the Tartars and the Turkomans into a vast Turanian Empire, which would stretch from the shores of the Mediterranean to the borders of China. Though the realization of such a scheme is exceedingly improbable, it is by no means as far-fetched or chimerical as it sounds, for Enver is bold, shrewd, highly intelligent and utterly unscrupulous and to weld the various races of his proposed empire he is utilizing an enormously effective agency—the fanatical faith of all Moslems in the future of Islam. Neither England nor France have any desire to stir up this hornet's nest, which would probably result in grave disorders among their own Moslem subjects and which would almost certainly precipitate widespread massacres of the Christians in Asia Minor, for the sake of dismembering Turkey and ousting the Sultan.

I have tried to make it clear that there is nothing which the Turks so urgently desire as for the United States to take a mandate for the whole of Turkey. Those who are in touch with public opinion in this country realize, of course, that the people of the United States would never approve of, and that Congress would never give its assent to such an adventure, yet there are a considerable number of well-informed, able and conscientious men—former Ambassador Henry Morgenthau and President Henry King of Oberlin, for example—who give it their enthusiastic support. And they are backed up by a host of missionaries, commercial representatives, concessionaires and special commissioners of one sort and another. When I was in Constantinople the European colony in that city was watching with interest and amusement the maneuvers of the Turks to bring the American officials around to accepting this view of the matter. They "rushed" the rear admiral who was acting as American High Commissioner and his wife as the members of a college fraternity "rush" a desirable freshman. And, come to think of it, most of the American officials who were sent out to investigate and report on conditions in Turkey are freshmen when it comes to the complexities of Near Eastern affairs. This does not apply, of course, to such men as Consul-General Ravndal at Constantinople, Consul-General Horton at Smyrna, Dr. Howard Bliss, President of the Syrian Protestant College at Beirut, and certain others, who have lived in the Levant for many years and are intimately familiar with the intricacies of its politics and the characters of its peoples. But it does apply to those officials who, after hasty and personally conducted tours through Asiatic Turkey, or a few months' residence in the Turkish capital, are accepted as "experts" by the Peace Conference and by the Government at Washington. When I listen to their dogmatic opinions on subjects of which most of them were in abysmal ignorance prior to the Armistice, I am always reminded of a remark once made to me by Sir Edwin Pears, the celebrated historian and authority on Turkish affairs. "I don't pretend to understand the Turkish character," Sir Edwin remarked dryly, "but, you see, I have lived here only forty years."

It is an interesting and altruistic scheme, this proposed regeneration at American expense of a corrupt and decadent empire, but in their enthusiasm its supporters seem to have overlooked several obvious objections. In the first place, though both England and France are perfectly willing to have the United States accept a mandate for European Turkey, Armenia and even Anatolia, I doubt if England would welcome with enthusiasm a proposal that she should evacuate Palestine and Mesopotamia, the conquest of which has cost her so much in blood and gold, or whether France would consent to renounce her claims to Syria, of which she has always considered herself the legatee. As for Italy and Greece, I imagine that it would prove as difficult to oust the one from Adalia and the other from Smyrna as it has been to oust the Poet from Fiume. Secondly, such a mandate would mean the end of Armenia's dream of independence, for, though she might be given a certain measure of autonomy, and though she would, of course, no longer be exposed to Turkish massacres, she would enjoy about as much real independence under such an arrangement as the native states of India enjoy under the British Raj. Lastly, nothing is further from our intention, if I know the temper of my countrymen, than to assume any responsibility in order to resurrect the Turk, nor are we interested in preserving the integrity of Turkey in any guise, shape or form. Instead of perpetuating the unspeakable rule of the Osmanli, we should assist in ending it forever.

And now we come to the question of accepting a mandate for Armenia. In order to get a mental picture of this foundling which we are asked to rear you must imagine a country about the size of North Dakota, with Dakota's cold winters and scorching summers, consisting of a dreary, monotonous, mile-high plateau with grass-covered, treeless mountains and watered by many rivers, whose valleys form wide strips of arable land. Rising above the general level of this Armenian tableland are barren and forbidding ranges, broken by many gloomy gorges, which culminate, on the extreme northeast, in the mighty peak of Ararat, the traditional resting-place of the Ark. Armenia is completely hemmed in by alien and potentially hostile races. On the northeast are the wild tribes of the Caucasus; on the east are the Persians, who, though not hostile to Armenian aspirations, are of the faith of Islam; along Armenia's southern border are the Kurds, a race as savage, as cruel and as relentless as were the Apaches of our own West; on the east is Anatolia, with its overwhelmingly Ottoman population. Before the war the Armenians in the six Turkish vilayets—Trebizond, Erzeroum, Van, Bitlis, Mamuret-el-Aziz and Diarbekir—numbered perhaps 2,000,000, as compared with about 700,000 Turks. But there is no saying how many Armenians remain, for during the past five years the Turks have perpetrated a series of wholesale massacres in order to be able to tell the Christian Powers, as a Turkish official cynically remarked, that "one cannot make a state without inhabitants."

As just and accurate an estimate of the Armenian character as any I have read is that written by Sir Charles William Wilson, perhaps the foremost authority on the subject, for the Encyclopædia Britannica: "The Armenians are essentially an Oriental people, possessing, like the Jews, whom they resemble in their exclusiveness and widespread dispersion, a remarkable tenacity of race and faculty of adaptation to circumstances. They are frugal, sober, industrious and intelligent and their sturdiness of character has enabled them to preserve their nationality and religion under the sorest trials. They are strongly attached to old manners and customs but have also a real desire for progress which is full of promise. On the other hand they are greedy of gain, quarrelsome in small matters, self-seeking and wanting in stability; and they are gifted with a tendency to exaggeration and a love of intrigue which has had an unfortunate effect on their history. They are deeply separated by religious differences and their mutual jealousies, their inordinate vanity, their versatility and their cosmopolitan character must always be an obstacle to a realization of the dreams of the nationalists. The want of courage and selfreliance, the deficiency in truth and honesty sometimes noticed in connection with them, are doubtless due to long servitude under an unsympathetic government."

It seems to me that it is time to subordinate sentiment to common sense in discussing the question of Armenia. I have known many Armenians and I have the deepest sympathy for the woes of that tragic race, but if the Armenians are in danger of extermination their fate is a matter for the Allies as a whole, or for the League of Nations, if there ever is one, but not for the United States alone. To administer and police Armenia would probably require an army corps, or upwards of 50,000 men, and I doubt if a force of such size could be raised for service in so remote and inhospitable a region without great difficulty. My personal opinion is that the Armenians, if given the necessary encouragement and assistance, are capable of governing themselves. Certainly they could not govern themselves more wretchedly than the Mexicans, yet there has been no serious proposal that the United States should take a mandate for Mexico. Everything considered, I am convinced that the highest interests of Armenia, of America, and of civilization would be best served by making Armenia an independent state, having much the same relation to the United States as Cuba. Let us finance the Armenian Republic by all means, let us lend it officers to organize its gendarmerie and teachers for its schools, let us send it agricultural and sanitary and building and financial experts, and let us give the rest of the world, particularly the Turks, to understand that we will tolerate no infringement of its sovereignly. Do that, set the Armenians on their feet, safeguard them politically and financially, and then leave them to work out their own salvation.

Though prophesying is a dangerous business, and likely to lead to embarrassment and chagrin for the prophet, I am willing to hazard a guess that the future maps of what was once the Ottoman Dominions will be laid out something after this fashion: Mesopotamia will be tinted red, because it will be British. Palestine will also be under Britain's ægis—a little independent Hebrew state, not much larger than Panama. Under the word "Syria" will appear the inscription "French Protectorate." The Adalia region will be designated "Italian Sphere of Influence," while Smyrna and its immediate hinterland will probably be labeled "Greek Sphere." Across the northeastern corner of Asia Minor will be spread the words "Republic of Armenia" and beneath, in parentheses, "Independence guaranteed by the United States." The whole of Anatolia, save the Greek and Italian fringes just mentioned, will be occupied and ruled by the Turks, for it is their ancestral home. The fortifications along the Dardanelles and the Bosphorus will be leveled and they, with Constantinople, will be under some form of international control, with equal rights for all nations. But, unless I am very much mistaken, the Turks will *not* be driven out of Europe, as has so long been predicted; the Ottoman Government will not retire to Brusa, in Asia Minor, but will continue to function in Stamboul, and the Sultan, as the religious head of Islam, will still dwell in the great white palace atop of Yildiz hill.

CHAPTER VI

WHAT THE PEACE-MAKERS HAVE DONE ON THE DANUBE

When I called upon M. Bratianu, the Prime Minister of Rumania, who was in Paris as a delegate to the Peace Conference, I opened the conversation by innocently remarking that I proposed to spend some weeks in his country during my travels in the Balkans. But I got no further, for M. Bratianu, whose tremendous shoulders and bristling black beard make him appear even larger than he is, sprang to his feet and brought his fist crashing down upon the table.

"You ought to know better than that, Major Powell," he angrily exclaimed. "Rumania is not in the Balkans and never has been. We object to being called a Balkan people."

I apologized for my slip, of course, and amicable relations were resumed, but I mention the incident as an illustration of how deeply the Rumanians resent the inclusion of their country in that group of turbulent kingdoms which compose what some one has aptly called the Cockpit of Europe. The Rumanians are as sensitive in this respect as are the haughty and aristocratic Creoles, inordinately proud of their French or Spanish ancestry, when some ignorant Northerner remarks that he had always supposed that Creoles were part negro. Not only is Rumania not one of the Balkan states, geographically speaking, but the Rumanians' idea of their country's importance has been enormously increased as a result of its recent territorial acquisitions, which have made it the sixth largest country in Europe, with an area very nearly equal to that of Italy and with a population three-fourths that of Spain. You were not aware, perhaps, that the width of Greater Rumania, from east to west, is as great as the width of France from the English Channel to the Mediterranean. One has to break into a run to keep pace with the march of geography these days.

Owing to the demoralization prevailing in Thrace and Bulgaria, railway communications between Constantinople and the Rumanian frontier were so disorganized that we decided to travel by steamer to

Constantza, taking the railway thence to Bucharest. Before the war the Royal Rumanian mail steamer *Carol I* was as trim and luxuriously fitted a vessel as one could have found in Levantine waters. For more than a year, however, she was in the hands of the Bolsheviks, so that when we boarded her her sides were red with rust, her cabins had been stripped of everything which could be carried away, and the straw-filled mattresses, each covered with a dubious-looking blanket, were as full of unwelcome occupants as the Black Sea was of floating mines.

THE RED BADGE OF MERCY IN THE BALKANS
American Red Cross women supplying food to a ship-load of starving Russian refugees at Constantza, Rumania

Constantza, the chief port of Rumania, is superbly situated on a headland overlooking the Black Sea. It has an excellent harbor, bordered on one side by a number of large grain elevators and on the other by a row of enormous petroleum tanks—the latter the property of an American corporation; a mile or so of asphalted streets, several surprisingly fine public buildings, and, on the beautifully terraced and landscaped waterfront, an imposing but rather ornate casino and many luxurious summer villas, most of which were badly damaged when the city was bombarded by the Bulgars. Constantza is a favorite seaside resort for Bucharest society and during the season its *plage* is thronged with summer visitors dressed in the height of the Paris fashion. From atop his marble pedestal in the city's principal square a statue of the Roman poet Ovid, who lived here in exile for many years, looks quizzically down upon the light-hearted throng.

It is in the neighborhood of 150 miles by railway from Constantza to Bucharest and before the war the Orient Express used to make the journey in less than four hours. Now it takes between twenty and thirty. We made a record trip, for our train left Constantza at four o'clock in the morning and pulled into Bucharest shortly before midnight. It is only fair to explain, however, that the length of time consumed in the journey was due to the fact that the bridge across the Danube near Tchernavoda, which was blown up by the Bulgars, had not been repaired, thus necessitating the transfer of the passengers and their luggage across the river on flat-boats, a proceeding which required several hours and was marked by the wildest confusion. So few trains are running in the Balkans that there are never enough, or nearly enough, seats to accommodate all the passengers, so that fully as many ride on the roofs of the coaches as inside. This has the advantage, in the eyes of the passengers, of making it impracticable for the conductor to collect the fares, but it also has certain disadvantages. During our trip from Constantza to Bucharest three roof passengers rolled off and were killed.

As a result of the lengthy occupation of the city by the Austro-Germans, and their systematic removal of machinery and industrial material of every description, everything is out of order in Bucharest. Water, electric lights, gas, telephones, elevators, street-cars *"ne marche pas."* Though we had a large and beautifully furnished room in the Palace Hotel we had to climb three flights of stairs to reach it, the light was furnished by candles, the water for the bathroom was brought in buckets, and, as the Germans had removed the wires of the house-telephones, we had to go into the hall and shout when we required a servant. Yet the almost total lack of conveniences does not deter the hotels from making the most exorbitant charges. Bucharest has always been an expensive city but to-day the prices are fantastic. At Capsa's, which is the most fashionable restaurant, it is difficult to get even a modest lunch for two for less than twelve dollars. But, notwithstanding the destruction of the nation's chief source of wealth, its oil wells, by the Rumanians themselves, in order to prevent their use by the enemy, and the systematic looting of the country by the invaders, there seems to be no lack of money in Bucharest, for the restaurants are filled to the doors nightly, there is a constant fusillade of champagne corks, and in the various gardens, all of which have cabaret performances, the popular dancers are showered with silver and notes. In fact, a customary evening in Bucharest is not very far removed, in its gaiety and abandon, from a New Year's Eve celebration in New York. Not even Paris can offer a gayer night life than the Rumanian capital, for at the Jockey Club it is no uncommon thing for 10,000 francs to change hands on the turn of a card or a whirl of the roulette wheel; out the Chaussée Kisselew, at the White City, the dance floor is crowded until daybreak with slender, rather effeminate-looking officers in beautiful uniforms of green or pale blue and superbly gowned and bejewelled women. Indeed, I doubt if there is any city of its size in the world on whose streets one sees so many *chic* and beautiful women, though I might add that their jewels are generally of a higher quality than their morals. As long as these bewitching beauties behave themselves they are not molested by the police, who seem to have an arrangement with the hotel managements looking toward their control. When Mrs. Powell and I arrived at our hotel the proprietor asked us for our passports, which, he explained, must be viséd by the police. The following morning my passport was returned alone.

"But where is my wife's passport?" I demanded, for in Southern Europe in these days it is impossible to travel even short distances without one's papers.

"But M'sieu must know that we always retain the lady's passport until he leaves," said the proprietor, with a knowing smile. "Then, should she disappear with M'sieu's watch, or his money, or his jewels, she will not be able to leave the city and the police can quickly arrest her. Yes, it is the custom here. A neat idea, *hein*?"

Though I succeeded in obtaining the return of Mrs. Powell's passport I am not at all certain that I succeeded in entirely convincing the *hôtelier* that she really was my wife.

Rumania is at present passing through a period of transition. Not only have the area and population of the country been more than doubled, but the war has changed all other conditions and the new forms of national life are still unsettled. In the summer of 1918 even the most optimistic Rumanians doubted if the nation would emerge from the war with more than a fraction of its former territory, yet today, as a result of the acquisition of Transylvania, Bessarabia and the eastern half of the Banat, the country's population has risen from seven to fourteen millions and its area from 50,000 to more than 100,000 square miles. The new conditions have brought new laws. Of these the most revolutionary is the law which forbids landowners to retain more than 1,000 acres of their land, the government taking over and paying for the residue, which is given to the peasants to cultivate. As a result of this policy, there have been practically no strikes or labor troubles in Rumania, for, now that most of their demands have been conceded, the Rumanian peasants seem willing to seek their welfare in work instead of Bolshevism. Heretofore the Jews, though liable to military service, have not been permitted a voice in the government of their country, but, as a result of recent legislation, they have now been granted full civil rights, though whether they will be permitted to exercise them is another question. The Jews, who number upwards of a quarter of a million, have a strangle hold on the finances of the country and they must not be permitted, the Rumanians insist, to get a similar grip on the nation's politics. It is only very recently, indeed, that Rumanian Jews have been granted passports, which meant that only those rich enough to obtain papers by bribery could enter or leave the country. The Rumanians with whom I discussed the question said quite frankly that the legislation granting suffrage to the Jews would probably be observed very much as the Constitutional Amendment granting suffrage to the negroes is observed in our own South.

The truth of the matter is that Rumania is in the hands of a clique of selfish and utterly unscrupulous politicians who have grown rich from their systematic exploitation of the national resources. Every bank and nearly every commercial enterprise of importance is in their hands. One of the present ministers entered the cabinet a poor man; to-day he is reputed to be worth twenty millions. Anything can be purchased in Rumania—passports, exemption from military service, cabinet portfolios, commercial concessions—if you have the money to pay for it. The fingers of Rumanian officials are as sticky as those of the Turks. An officer of the American Relief Administration told me that barely sixty per cent, of the supplies sent from the United States for the relief of the Rumanian peasantry ever reached those for whom they were intended; the other forty per cent, was kept by various officials. To find a parallel for the political corruption which exists throughout Rumania it is necessary to go back to New York under the Tweed administration or to Mexico under the Diaz régime.

From a wealthy Hungarian landowner, with whom I traveled from Bucharest to the frontier of Jugoslavia, I obtained a graphic idea of what can be accomplished by money in Rumania. This young Hungarian, who had been educated in England and spoke with a Cambridge accent, possessed large estates in northeastern Hungary. After four years' service as an officer of cavalry he was demobilized upon the signing of the Armistice. When the revolution led by Bela Kun broke out in Budapest he escaped from that city on foot, only to be arrested by the Rumanians as he was crossing the Rumanian frontier. Fortunately for him, he had ample funds in his possession, obtained from the sale of the cattle on his estate, so that he was able to purchase his freedom after spending only three days in jail. But his release did not materially improve his situation, for he had no passport and, as Hungary was then under Bolshevist rule, he was unable to obtain one. And he realized that without a passport it would be impossible for him to join his wife and children, who were awaiting him in Switzerland. As luck would have it, however, he was slightly acquainted with the prefect of a small town in Transylvania—for obvious reasons I shall not mention its name—which he finally reached after great difficulty, traveling by night and lying hidden by day so as to avoid being halted and questioned by the Rumanian patrols. By paying the prefect 1,000 francs and giving him and his friends a dinner at the local hotel, he obtained a certificate stating that he was a citizen of the town and in good standing with the local authorities. Armed with this document, which was sufficient to convince inquisitive border officials of his Rumanian nationality, he took train for Bucharest, where he spent five weeks dickering for a Rumanian passport which would enable him to leave the country. Including the bribes and entertainments which he gave to officials, and gifts of one sort and another to minor functionaries, it cost him something over 25,000 francs to obtain a passport duly viséd for Switzerland. But my friend's anxieties did not end there, for a Rumanian leaving the country was not permitted to take more than 1,000 francs in currency with him, those suspected of having in their possession funds in excess of this amount being subjected to a careful search at the frontier. My friend had with him, however, something over 500,000 francs, all that he had been able to realize from his estates. How to get this sum out of the country was a perplexing problem, but he finally solved it by concealing the notes, which were of large denomination, in the bottom of a box of expensive face powder, which, he explained to the officials at the frontier, he was taking as a present to his wife. When the train drew into the first Serbian station and he realized that he was beyond the reach of pursuit, he capered up and down the platform like a small boy when school closes for the long vacation.

Considerable astonishment seems to have been manifested by the American press and public at the disinclination of Rumania and Jugoslavia to sign the treaty with Austria without reservations. Yet this should scarcely occasion surprise, for the attitude of the great among the Allies toward the smaller brethren who helped them along the road to victory has been at times blameworthy, often inexplicable, and on frequent occasions arrogant and tactless. At the outset of the Peace Conference some endeavor was made to live up to the promises so loudly made that henceforth the rights of the weak were to receive as much attention as those of the strong. Commissions were formed to study various aspects of the questions involved in the peace and upon these the representatives of the smaller nations were given seats. But this did not last long. Within a month Messrs. Wilson, Lloyd-George, Clémenceau and Orlando had made themselves virtually the dictators of the Peace Conference, deciding behind closed doors matters of vital moment to the national welfare of the small states without so much as taking them into consultation. Prime Minister Bratianu, who went to Paris as the head of the Rumanian peace delegation, told me, his voice hoarse with indignation, that the "Big Four," in settling Rumania's future boundaries, had not only not consulted him but that he had not even been informed of the terms decided upon. "They hand us a fountain pen and say 'Sign here,'" the Premier exclaimed, "and then they are surprised if we refuse to affix our signatures to a document which vitally concerns our national future but about which we have never been consulted."

We Americans, of all peoples, should realize that a small nation is as jealous of its independence as a large one. As a matter of fact, Rumania and her sister-states of Southeastern Europe, who still bear the scars of Turkish oppression, are super-sensitive in this respect, the fact that they have so often been the victims of intriguing neighbors making them more than ordinarily suspicious and resentful toward any action which tends to limit their mastery of their own households. Hence they regard that clause of the Treaty of St. Germain providing for the protection of ethnical minorities with an indignation which cannot easily be appreciated by the Western nations. The boundaries of the new and aggrandized states of Southeastern Europe will necessarily include alien minorities—this cannot be avoided—and the Peace Conference held that the welfare of such minorities must be the special concern of the League of Nations. Take the case of Rumania, for example. In order to unite her people she must annex some compact masses of aliens which, in certain cases at least, have been deliberately planted within ethnological frontiers for a specific purpose. The settlements of Magyars in Transylvania, who, under Hungarian rule, were permitted to exploit their Rumanian neighbors without let or hindrance, will not willingly surrender the privileges they have so long enjoyed and submit to a régime of strict justice and equality. On the other hand, Rumania can scarcely be expected to agree to an arrangement which would not only impair her sovereignty but would almost certainly encourage intrigue and unrest among these alien minorities. How would the United States regard a proposal to submit its administration of the Philippines to international control? How would England like the League of Nations to take a hand in the government of Ireland? That, briefly stated, is the reason why both Rumania and Jugoslavia objected so strongly to the inclusion of the so-called racial minorities clause in the Treaty of St. Germain. Looking at the other side of the question, it Is easy to understand the solicitude which the treaty-makers at Paris displayed for the thousands of Magyars, Serbs and Bulgars who, without so much as a by-your-leave, they have placed under Rumanian rule. No less authority than Viscount Bryce has made the assertion that in Transylvania alone (which, by the way, has an area considerably greater than all our New England states put together), which has been taken over by Rumania, fully a third of the population has no affinity with the Rumanians. Similarly, there are whole towns in the Dobrudja which are composed of Bulgarians, there are large groups of Russian Slavs in Bessarabia, and considerable colonies of Jugoslavs in the eastern half of the Banat which, very much against their wishes, have been forced to submit to Rumanian rule. Whether, now that the tables are turned, the Rumanians will put aside their ancient animosities and prejudices and give these new and unwilling citizens every privilege which they themselves enjoy, is a question which only the future can solve.

Another question, which has agitated Rumania even more violently than that of the racial minorities clause, was the demand made by the Great Powers that the Rumanian army be withdrawn from Hungary and that the livestock and agricultural implements of which that unhappy country was stripped by the Rumanian forces be immediately returned. Here is the Rumanian version: Hungary went Bolshevist and assumed a hostile attitude toward Rumania, Czechoslovakia and Jugoslavia, the three countries which will benefit by her dismemberment according to the principle of nationality. Hungary attacked these countries by arms and by anarchistic propaganda. The Rumanians, the Czechoslovaks and the Jugoslavs, wishing to defend themselves, asked permission of the Supreme Council to deal drastically with the Hungarian menace. The reply, which was late in coming, was couched in vague and unsatisfactory language. Emboldened by the vacillatory attitude of the Powers, the Hungarians began a military offensive, invading Czechoslovakia and crossing the lines of the Armistice in Rumania and Jugoslavia. In order to prevent a spread of this Bolshevist movement the three countries prepared to occupy Hungary with troops, whereupon a command came from the Supreme Council in Paris that such aggression would not be tolerated. This encouraged Bela Kun, the Hungarian Trotzky, and made him so popular that he succeeded in raising a Red army with which he crossed the River

Theiss and invaded Rumania. Whereupon the Rumanian army, being unable to obtain support from the Supreme Council, pushed back the Hungarians, occupied Budapest, overthrew Bela Kun's administration and restored order in Hungary. But the Supreme Council, feeling that its authority had been ignored by the little country, sent several messages to the Rumanian Government peremptorily ordering it to withdraw its troops immediately from Hungary. Here endeth the Rumanian version.

Now the real reason which actuated the Supreme Council was not that it felt that its authority had been slighted, but because it was informed by its representatives in Hungary that the Rumanians had not stopped with ousting Bela Kun and suppressing Bolshevism, but were engaged in systematically looting the country, driving off thousands of head of livestock, and carrying away all the machinery, rolling stock, telephone and telegraph wires and instruments and metalwork they could lay their hands on, thereby completely crippling the industries of Hungary and depriving great numbers of people of employment. The Rumanians retorted that the Austro-German armies had systematically looted Rumania during their three years of occupation and that they were only taking back what belonged to them. The Hungarians, while admitting that Rumania had been pretty thoroughly stripped of animals and machinery by von Mackensen's armies, asserted that this loot had not remained in Hungary but had been taken to Germany, which was probably true. The Supreme Council took the position that the animals and material which the Rumanians were rushing out of Hungary in train-loads was not the sole property of Rumania, but that it was the property of all the Allies, and that the Supreme Council would apportion it among them in its own good time. The Council pointed out, furthermore, that if the Rumanians succeeded in wrecking Hungary industrially, as they were evidently trying to do, it would be manifestly impossible for the Hungarians to pay any war indemnity whatsoever. And finally, that a bankrupt and starving Hungary meant a Bolshevist Hungary and that there was already enough trouble of that sort in Eastern Europe without adding to it. The Rumanians proving deaf to these arguments, the Supreme Council sent three messages, one after the other, to the Bucharest government, ordering the immediate withdrawal from Hungarian soil of the Rumanian troops. Yet the Rumanian troops remained in Budapest and the looting of Hungary continued, the Rumanian government declaring that the messages had never been received. Meanwhile every one in the kingdom, from Premier to peasant, was laughing in his sleeve at the helplessness of the Supreme Council. But they laughed too soon. For the Supreme Council wired to the Food Administrator, Herbert Hoover, who was in Vienna, informing him of the facts of the situation, whereupon Mr. Hoover, who has a blunt and uncomfortably direct way of achieving his ends, sent a curt message to the Rumanian government informing it that, if the orders of the Supreme Council were not immediately obeyed, he would shut off its supplies of food. *That* message produced action. The troops were withdrawn. I can recall no more striking example of the amazing changes brought about in Europe by the Great War than the picture of this boyish-faced Californian mining engineer coolly giving orders to a European government, and having those orders promptly obeyed, after the commands of the Great Powers had been met with refusal and derision. To take a slight liberty with the lines of Mr. Kipling—

> *"The Kings must come down and the Emperors frown*
> *When Herbert Hoover says 'Stop!'"*

Up to that time the United States had been immensely popular in Rumania. But Mr. Hoover's action made us about as popular with the Rumanians as the smallpox. He and we were charged with being actuated by the most despicable and sordid motives. The King himself told me that he was convinced that Mr. Hoover was in league with certain great commercial interests which wished to take their revenge for their failure to obtain commercial concessions of great value in Rumania. A cabinet minister, in discussing the incident with me, became so inarticulate with rage that he could scarcely talk at all.

But the United States is not the only country which has lost the confidence of the Rumanians. France is even more deeply distrusted and disliked than we are. And this in spite of the fact that the upper classes of Rumania have held up the French as their ideal for the past fifty years. Indeed, wealthy Rumanians live in a fashion more French than if they dwelt in Paris itself. This sudden unpopularity of the French is due to several causes. After having expected much of them, the people were amazed and bitterly disappointed at their apparent indifference toward the future of Rumania. Then there were the unfortunate incidents at Odessa, the withdrawal of the French forces from that city before the advance of the Bolsheviks, and the regrettable happening in the French Black Sea fleet These things, of course, contributed to loss of French prestige. Another contributory factor has been the lack of enterprise of French capitalists, causing those who control the financial and economic development of Rumania to seek encouragement and assistance elsewhere. But the underlying reason for the deep-seated distrust of France is to be found, I think, in France's attempt to maintain the balance of power in Southeastern Europe by building up a strong Jugoslavia. Now the Rumanians, it must be remembered, hate the Jugoslavs even more bitterly than they hate the Hungarians—and they are far more afraid of them. This hatred is not merely the result of the age-long antagonism between the Latin and the Slav; it is also political. The Rumanians have watched with growing jealousy and apprehension the expansion of Serbia into a state with a population and area nearly equal to their own. After having long dreamed of the day when they would themselves be arbiters of the destinies of the nations of Southeastern Europe, they see their political supremacy challenged by the new Kingdom of the Serbs, Croats and Slovenes, behind which they discern the power and influence of France. When the dismemberment of the Austro-Hungarian Empire began, Rumania demanded and expected the whole of the great rich province of the Banat, with the Maros River for her northern and the Danube for her southern frontier.

"But that would place our capital within range of the Rumanian artillery," the Serbian prime minister is said to have exclaimed.

"Then move your capital," the Rumanian premier responded drily.

As a result of this controversy over the Banat the relations of the two nations have been strained almost to the breaking-point. When I was in the Banat in the autumn of 1919 the Rumanian and Serbian frontier guards were glowering at each other like fighting terriers held in leash, and the slightest untoward incident would have precipitated a conflict! Although, by the terms of the Treaty of St. Germain, Jugoslavia was awarded the western half of the Banat, Rumania is prepared to take advantage of the first opportunity which presents itself to take it away from her rival. When I was in Bucharest a cabinet minister concluded a lengthy exposition of Rumania's position by declaring:

"Within the next two or three years, in all probability, there will be a war between Jugoslavia and Italy over the Dalmatian question. The day that Jugoslavia goes to war with Italy we will attack Jugoslavia and seize the Banat. The Danube is Rumania's natural and logical frontier."

This would seem to bear out the assertion that there exists a secret alliance between Italy and Rumania, which, if true, would place Jugoslavia in the unhappy position of a nut between the jaws of a cracker. I have also been told on excellent authority that there is likewise an "understanding" between Italy and Bulgaria that, should the former become engaged in a war with the Jugoslavs, the latter will attack the Serbs from the east and regain her lost provinces in Macedonia. A pleasant prospect for Southeastern Europe, truly.

While we were in Bucharest we received an invitation—"command" is the correct word according to court usage—to visit the King and Queen of Rumania at their Château of Pelesch, near Sinaia, in the Carpathians. It is about a hundred miles by road from the capital to Sinaia and the first half of the journey, which we made by motor, was over a road as execrable as any we found in the Balkans. Upon reaching the foothills of the Carpathians, however, the highway, which had been steadily growing worse, suddenly took a turn for the better—due, no doubt, to the invigorating qualities of the mountain atmosphere—and climbed vigorously upward through wild gorges and splendid pine forests which reminded me of the Adirondacks of Northern New York. Notwithstanding the atrocious condition of the highway, which constantly threatened to dislocate our joints as well as those of the car, and the choking, blinding clouds of yellow dust, every change of figure on the speedometer brought new and interesting scenes. For mile after mile the road, straight as though marked out by a ruler, ran between fields of wheat and corn as vast as those of our own West. In spite of the fact that the Austro-Germans carried off all the animals and farming implements they could lay their hands on, the agricultural prosperity of Rumania is astounding. In 1916, for example, while involved in a terribly destructive war, Rumania produced more wheat than Minnesota and about twenty-five times as much corn as our three Pacific Coast states combined. At frequent intervals we passed huge scarlet threshing machines, most of them labeled "Made in U.S.A.," which were centers of activity for hundreds of white-smocked peasants who were hauling in the grain with ox-teams, feeding it into the voracious maws of the machines, and piling the residue of straw into the largest stacks I have ever seen. As we drew near the mountains the grain fields gave way to grazing lands where great herds of cattle of various breeds—brindled milch animals, massive cream-colored oxen, blue-gray buffalo with elephant like hides and broad, curving horns, and gaunt steers that looked for all the world like Texas longhorns—browsed amid the lush green grass.

Though the villages of the Wallachian plain are few and far between, and though it is no uncommon thing for a peasant to walk a dozen miles from his home to the fields in which he works, the whole region seemed a-hum with industry. The Rumanian peasant, like his fellows below the Danube, is, as a rule, a good-natured, easy-going though easily excited, reasonably honest and extremely industrious fellow who labors from dawn to darkness in six days of the week and spends the seventh in harmless village carouses, chiefly characterized by dancing, music and the cheap native wine. Rumania is one of the few countries in Europe where the peasants still dress like the pictures on the postcards. The men wear curly-brimmed shovel hats of black felt, like those affected by English curates, and loose shirts of white linen, whose tails, instead of being tucked into the trousers, flap freely about their legs, giving them the appearance of having responded to an alarm of fire without waiting to finish dressing. On Sundays and holidays men and women alike[4] appear in garments covered with the gorgeous needlework for which Rumania is famous, some of the women's dresses being so heavily embroidered in gold and silver that from a little distance the wearers look as though they were enveloped in chain mail. A considerable and undesirable element of Rumania's population consists of gipsies, whence their name of Romany, or Rumani. The Rumanian gipsies, who are nomads and vagrants like their kinsmen in the United States, are generally lazy, quarrelsome, dishonest and untrustworthy, supporting themselves by horse-trading and cattle-stealing or by their flocks and herds. We stopped near one of their picturesque encampments in order to repair a tire and I took a picture of a young woman with a child in her arms, but when I declined to pay her the five lei she demanded for the privilege, she flew at me like an angry cat, screaming curses and maledictions. But her picture was not worth five lei, as you can see for yourself.

THE GYPSY WHO DEMANDED FIVE LEI FOR THE PRIVILEGE OF TAKING HER PICTURE

The Castle of Pelesch is just such a royal residence as Anthony Hope has depicted in *The Prisoner of Zenda*. It gives the impression, at first sight, of a confusion of turrets, gables, balconies, terraces, parapets and fountains, but one quickly forgets its architectural shortcomings in the beauty of its surroundings. It stands amid velvet lawns and wonderful rose gardens in a sort of forest glade, from which the pine-clothed slopes of the Carpathians rise steeply on every side, the beam-and-plaster walls, the red-tiled roofs, and the blazing gardens of the château forming a striking contrast to the austerity of the mountains and the solemnity of the encircling forest.

A PEA SANT OF OLD SERBIA
The Serbian peasant is simple, kindly, hospitable, honest, and generous, and, though he could not be described ... as a hard worker, his wife invariably is

We had rather expected to be presented to Queen Marie with some semblance of formality in one of the reception rooms of the château, but she sent word by her lady-in-waiting that she would receive us in the gardens. A few minutes later she came swinging toward us across a great stretch of rolling lawn, a splendid figure of a woman, dressed in a magnificent native costume of white and silver, a white scarf partially concealing her masses of tawny hair, a long-bladed poniard in a silver sheath hanging from her girdle. At her heels were a dozen Russian wolf hounds, the gift, so she told me, of the Grand Duke Nicholas, the former commander-in-chief of the Russian armies. I have seen many queens, but I have never seen one who so completely meets the popular conception of what a queen should look like as Marie of Rumania. Though in the middle forties, her complexion is so faultless, her physique so superb, her presence so commanding that, were she utterly unknown, she would still be a center of attraction in any assemblage. Had she not been born to a crown she would almost certainly have made a great name for herself, probably as an actress. She paints exceptionally well and has written several successful books and stories, thereby following the example of her famous predecessor on the Rumanian throne, Queen Elizabeth, better known as Carmen Sylva. She speaks English like an Englishwoman, as well she may, for she is a granddaughter of Queen Victoria. She is also a descendant of the Romanoffs, for one of her grandfathers was Alexander III of Russia. In her manner she is more simple and democratic than many American women that I know, her poise and simplicity being in striking contrast to the manners of two of my countrywomen who had spent the night preceding our arrival at the castle and who were manifestly much impressed by this contact with the Lord's Anointed. When luncheon was announced her second daughter, Princess Marie, had not put in an appearance. But, instead of despatching the major domo to inform her Royal Highness that the meal was served, the Queen stepped to the foot of the great staircase and called, "Hurry up, Mignon. You're keeping us all waiting," whereupon a voice replied from the upper regions, "All right, mamma. I'll be down in a minute." Not much like the picture of palace life that the novelists and the motion-picture playwrights give us, is it? I might add that the Queen commonly refers to the plump young princess as "Fatty," a nickname which she hardly deserves, however. In her conversations with me the Queen was at times almost disconcertingly frank. "Royalty is going out of fashion," she remarked on one occasion, "but I like my job and I'm going to do everything I can to keep it." To Mrs. Powell she said, "I have beauty, intelligence and executive ability. I would be successful in life if I were not a queen."

Unlike many persons who occupy exalted positions, she has a real sense of humor.

"Yesterday," she remarked, "was Nicholas's birthday," referring to her second son, Prince Nicholas, who, since his elder brother, Prince Carol, renounced his rights to the throne in order to marry the girl he loved, has become the heir apparent. "At breakfast his father remarked, 'I'm sorry, Nicholas, but I haven't any birthday present for you. The shops in Bucharest were pretty well cleaned out by the Germans, you know, and I didn't remember your birthday in time to send to Paris for a present.' 'Do you really wish to give Nicholas a present, Nando?' (the diminutive of Ferdinand) I asked him. 'Of course I do,' the King answered, 'but what is there to give him?' 'That's the easiest thing in the world,' I replied. 'There is nothing that would give Nicholas so much pleasure as an engraving of his dear father—on a thousand-franc note.'"

Prince Nicholas, the future king of Rumania, who is being educated at Eton, looks and acts like any normal American "prep" school boy.

"Do the boys still wear top hats at Eton?" I asked him.

"Yes, they do," he answered, "but it's a silly custom. And they cost two guineas apiece. I leave it to you, Major, if two guineas isn't too much for any hat."

When I told him that in democratic America certain Fifth Avenue hatters charge the equivalent of five guineas for a bowler he looked at me in frank unbelief. "But then," he remarked, "all Americans are rich."

Shortly before luncheon we were joined by King Ferdinand, a slenderly built man, somewhat under medium height, with a grizzled beard, a genial smile and merry, twinkling eyes. He wore the gray-green field uniform and gold-laced kepi of a Rumanian general, the only thing about his dress which suggested his exalted rank being the insignia of the Order of Michael the Brave, which hung from his neck by a gold-and-purple ribbon. Were you to see him in other clothes and other circumstances you might well mistake him for an active and successful professional man. King Ferdinand is the sort of man one enjoys chatting with in front of an open fire over the cigars, for, in addition to being a shrewd judge of men and events and having a remarkably exact knowledge of world affairs, he possesses in an altogether exceptional degree the qualities of tact, kindliness and humor.

The King did not hesitate to express his indignation that the re-making of the map of Europe should have been entrusted to men who possessed so little first-hand knowledge of the nations whose boundaries they were re-shaping.

"A few days before the signing of the Treaty of St. Germain," he told me, "Lloyd George sent for one of the experts attached to the Peace Conference.

"'Where is this Banat that Rumania and Serbia are quarreling over?' he inquired.

"'I will show you, sir,' the attaché answered, unrolling a map of southeastern Europe. For several minutes he explained in detail to the British Premier the boundaries of the Banat and the conflicting territorial claims to which its division had given rise. But when he paused Lloyd George made no response. He was sound asleep!

"Yet a little group of men," the King continued, "who know no more about the nations whose destinies they are deciding than Lloyd George knew about the Banat, have abrogated to themselves the right to cut up and apportion territories as casually as though they were dividing apple-tarts."

The New Frontiers of Freedom: From the Alps to the Aegean

KING FERDINAND TELLS MRS. POWELL HIS OPINION OF THE FASHION IN WHICH THE PEACE CONFERENCE TREATED RUMANIA, WHILE QUEEN MARIE LISTENS APPROVINGLY

The impression prevails in other countries that it is Queen Marie who is really the head of the Rumanian royal family and that the King is little more than a figurehead. With this estimate I do not agree. Rumania could have no better spokesman than Queen Marie, whose talents, beauty, and exceptional tact peculiarly fit her for the difficult rôle she has been called upon to play. But the King, though he is by nature quiet and retiring, is by no means lacking in political sagacity or the courage of his convictions, being, I am convinced, as important a factor in the government of his country as the limitations of its constitution permit. Though none too well liked, I imagine, by the professional politicians, who in Rumania, as in other countries, resent any attempt at interference by the sovereign with their plans, the royal couple are immensely popular with the masses of the people, Ferdinand frequently being referred to as "the peasants' King." In the darkest days of the war, when Rumania was overrun by the enemy and it seemed as though Moldavia and the northern Dobrudja were all that could be saved to the nation, King Ferdinand and Queen Marie, instead of escaping from their country or asking the enemy for terms, retreated with the army to Jassy, on the easternmost limits of the kingdom, where they underwent the horrors of that terrible winter with their soldiers, the King serving with the troops in the field and the Queen working in the hospitals as a Red Cross nurse. Less than three years later, however, on November twentieth, 1919, there assembled in Bucharest the first parliament of Greater Rumania, attended by deputies from all those Rumanian regions—Bessarabia, Transylvania, the Banat, the Bucovina and the Dobrudja—which had been restored to the Rumanian motherland. At the head of the chamber, in the great gilt chair of state, sat Ferdinand I, who, from the fugitive ruler, shivering with his ragged soldiers in the frozen marshes beside the Pruth, has become the sovereign of a country having the sixth largest population in Europe and has taken his place in Rumanian history beside Stephen the Great and Michael the Brave as Ferdinand the Liberator.

CHAPTER VII

MAKING A NATION TO ORDER

From the young officers who wore on their shoulders the silver greyhound of the American Courier Service we heard many discouraging tales of the annoyances and discomforts for which we must be prepared in traveling through Hungary, the Banat and Jugoslavia. But, to tell the truth, I did not take these warnings very seriously, for I had observed that a profoundly pessimistic attitude of mind characterized all of the Americans or English whose duties had kept them in the Balkans for any length of time. In Salonika this mental condition was referred to as "the Balkan tap"—derived, no doubt, from the verb "to knock," as with a hammer—and it usually implied that those suffering from the ailment had outstayed their period of usefulness and should be sent home.

Thrice weekly a train composed of an assortment of ramshackle and dilapidated coaches, called by courtesy the Orient Express, which maintained an average speed of fifteen miles an hour, left Bucharest for Vincovce, a small junction town in the Banat, where it was supposed to make connections with the south-bound Simplon Express from Paris to Belgrade and with the north-bound express from Belgrade to Paris. The Simplon Express likewise ran thrice weekly, so, if the connections were missed at Vincovce, the passengers were compelled to spend at least two days in a small Hungarian town which was notorious, even in that region, for its discomforts and its dirt. All went well with us, however, the train at one time attaining the dizzy speed of thirty miles an hour, until, in a particularly desolate portion of the great Hungarian plain, we came to an abrupt halt. When, after a half hour's wait, I descended to ascertain the cause of the delay, I found the train crew surrounded by a group of indignant and protesting passengers.

"What's the trouble?" I inquired.

"The engineer claims that he has run out of coal," some one answered. "But he says that there is a coal depot three or four kilometers ahead and that, if each first-class passenger will contribute fifty francs, and each second-class passenger twenty francs, he figures that it will enable him to buy just enough coal to reach Vincovce. Otherwise, he says, we will probably miss both connections, which means that we must stay in Vincovce for forty-eight hours. And if you had ever seen Vincovce you would understand that such a prospect is anything but alluring."

While my fellow-passengers were noisily debating the question I strolled ahead to take a look at the engine. As I had been led to expect from the stories I had heard from the courier officers, the tender contained an ample supply of coal—enough, it seemed to me, to haul the train to Trieste.

"This is nothing but a hold-up," I told the assembled passengers. "There is plenty of coal in the tender. I am as anxious to make the connection as any of you, but I will settle here and raise bananas, or whatever they do raise in the Banat, before I will submit to this highwayman's demands."

Seeing that his bluff had been called, the engineer, favoring me with a murderous glance, sullenly climbed into his cab and the train started, only to stop again, however, a few miles further on, this time, the engineer explained, because the engine had broken down. There being no way of disputing this statement, it became a question of pay or stay—and we stayed. The engineer did not get his tribute and we did not get our train at Vincovce, where we spent twenty hot, hungry and extremely disagreeable hours before the arrival of a local train bound for Semlin, across the Danube from Belgrade. We completed our journey to the Jugoslav capital in a fourth-class compartment into which were already squeezed two Serbian soldiers, eight peasants, a crate of live poultry and a dog, to say nothing of a multitude of small and undesired occupants whose presence caused considerable annoyance to every one, including the dog. We were glad when the train arrived at Semlin.

Late in the summer of 1919, as a result of the reconstruction of the railway bridges which had been blown up by the Bulgarians early in the war, through service between Salonika and Belgrade was restored. As the journey consumed from three to five days, however, the train stopping for the night at stations where the hotel accommodation was of the most impossible description, the American and British officials and relief-workers who were compelled to make the journey (I never heard of any one making it for pleasure) usually hired a freight car, which they fitted up with army cots and a small cook-stove, thus traveling in comparative comfort.

Curiously enough, the only trains running on anything approaching a schedule in the Balkans were those loaded with Swiss goods and belonging to the Swiss Government. In crossing Southern Hungary we passed at least half-a-dozen of them, they being readily distinguished by a Swiss flag painted on each car. Each train, consisting of forty cars, was accompanied by a Swiss officer and twenty infantrymen—finely set-up fellows in *feldgrau* with steel helmets modeled after the German pattern. Had the trains not been thus guarded, I was told, the goods would never have reached their destination and the cars, which are the property of the Swiss State Railways, would never have been returned. It is by such drastic methods as this that Switzerland, though hard hit by the war, has kept the wheels of her industries turning and her currency from serious depreciation. I have rarely seen more hopeless-looking people than those congregated on the platforms of the little stations at which we stopped in Hungary. The Rumanian armies had swept the country clean of livestock and agricultural machinery, throwing thousands of peasants out of work, and, owing to the appalling depreciation of the kroner, which was worth less than a twentieth of its normal value, great numbers of people who, under ordinary conditions, would have been described as comfortably well off, found themselves with barely sufficient resources to keep themselves from want. To add to their discouragement, the greatest uncertainty prevailed as to Hungary's future. In order to obtain an idea of just how familiar the inhabitants of the rural districts were with political conditions, I asked four intelligent-looking men in succession who was the ruler of Hungary and what was its present form of government. The first opined that the Archduke Joseph had been chosen king; another ventured the belief that the country was a republic with Bela Kun as president; the third asserted that Hungary had been annexed to Rumania; while the last man I questioned said quite frankly that he didn't know who was running the country, or what its form of government was, and that he didn't much care. As a result of the decision of the Peace Conference which awarded Transylvania to Rumania and divided the Banat between Rumania and Jugoslavia, Hungary finds herself stripped of virtually all her forests, all her mines, all her oil wells, and all of her manufactories save those in Budapest, thus stripping the bankrupt and demoralized nation of practically all of her resources save her wheat-fields. I talked with a number of Americans and English who were conversant with Hungary's internal condition and they agreed that it was doubtful if the country, stripped of its richest territories, deprived of most of its resources, and hemmed in by hostile and jealous peoples, could long exist as an independent state. On several occasions I heard the opinion expressed that sooner or later the Hungarians, in order to save themselves from complete ruin, would ask to be admitted to the Jugoslav Confederation, thereby obtaining for their products an outlet to the sea. In any event, the Hungarians appear to have a more friendly feeling for their Jugoslav neighbors than for the Rumanians, whom they charge with a deliberate attempt to bring about their economic ruin.

In spite of the prohibitive cost of labor and materials, we found that the traces of the Austrian bombardment of Belgrade in 1914, which did enormous damage to the Serbian capital, were rapidly being effaced and that the city was fast resuming its pre-war appearance. The place was as busy as a boom town in the oil country. The Grand Hotel, where the food was the best and cheapest we found in the Balkans, was filled to the doors with officers, politicians, members of parliament—for the Skupshtina was in session—relief workers, commercial travelers and concession seekers, and the huge Hotel Moskowa, built, I believe, with Russian capital, was about to reopen. Architecturally, Belgrade shows many traces of Muscovite influence, many of the more important buildings having the ornate façades of pink, green and purple tiles, the colored glass windows, and the gilded domes which are so characteristically Russian. Though the main thoroughfare of the city, formerly called the Terásia but now known as Milan Street, is admirably paved with wooden blocks, the cobble pavements of the other streets have remained unchanged since the days of Turkish rule, being so rough that it is almost impossible to drive a motor car over them without imminent danger of breaking the springs. Five minutes' walk from the center of the city, on a promontory commanding a superb view of the Danube and its junction with the Save, is a really charming park known as the Slopes of Dreaming, where, on fine evenings, almost the entire population of the capital appears to be promenading, the rather drab appearance of an urban crowd being brightened by the gaily embroidered costumes of the peasants and the silver-trimmed uniforms of the Serbian officers.

THE WINE-SHOP WHICH IS POINTED OUT TO VISITORS AS "THE CRADLE OF THE WAR"

The palace known as the Old Konak, where King Alexander and Queen Draga were assassinated under peculiarly revolting circumstances on the night of June 11, 1905, and from an upper window of which their mutilated bodies were thrown into the garden, has been torn down, presumably because of its unpleasant associations for the present dynasty, but only a stone's throw away from the tragic spot is being erected a large and ornate palace of gray stone, ornamented with numerous carvings, as a residence for Prince-Regent Alexander, who, when I was there, was occupying a modest one-story building on the opposite side of the street. By far the most interesting building in Belgrade, however, is a low, tile-roofed, white-walled wine-shop at the corner of Knes Mihajelowa Uliza and Kolartsch Uliza, which is pointed out to visitors as "the Cradle of the War," for in the low-ceilinged room on the second floor is said to have been hatched the plot which resulted in the assassination of the Austrian archducal couple at Serajevo in the spring of 1914 and thereby precipitated Armageddon.

In this connection, here is a story, told me by a Czechoslovak who had served as an officer in the Serbian army during the war, which throws an interesting sidelight on the tragedy of Serajevo. This officer's uncle, a colonel in the Austrian army, had been, it seemed, equerry to the Archduke Ferdinand, being in attendance on the Archduke at the Imperial shooting-lodge in Bohemia when, early in the spring of 1914, the German Emperor, accompanied by Admiral von Tirpitz, went there, ostensibly for the shooting. The day after their arrival, according to my informant's story, the Emperor and the Archduke went out with the guns, leaving Admiral von Tirpitz at the lodge with the Archduchess. The equerry, who was on duty in an anteroom, through a partly opened door overheard the Admiral urging the Archduchess to obtain the consent of her husband — with whom she was known to exert extraordinary influence — to a union of Austria-Hungary with Germany upon the death of Francis Joseph, who was then believed to be dying — a scheme which had long been cherished by the Kaiser and the Pan-Germans.

"Never will I lend my influence to such a plan!" the equerry heard the Archduchess violently exclaim. "Never! Never! Never!"

At the moment the Emperor and the Archduke, having returned from their battue, entered the room, whereupon the Archduchess, her voice shrill with indignation, poured out to her husband the story of von Tirpitz's proposal. The Archduke, always noted for the violence of his temper, promptly sided with his wife, angrily accusing the Kaiser of intriguing behind his back against the independence of Austria. Ensued a violent altercation between the ruler of Germany and the Austrian heir-apparent, which ended in the Kaiser and his adviser abruptly terminating their visit and departing the same evening for Berlin.

For the truth of this story I do not vouch; I merely repeat it in the words in which it was told to me by an officer whose veracity I have no reason to question. There are many things which point to its probability. Certain it is that the Archduke, who was a man of strong character and passionately devoted to the best interests of the Dual Monarchy, was the greatest obstacle to the Kaiser's scheme for the union of the two empires under his rule, a scheme which, could it have been realized, would have given Germany that highroad to the East and that outlet to the Warm Water of which the Pan-Germans had long dreamed. The assassination of the Archduke a few weeks later not only removed the greatest stumbling-block to these schemes of Teutonic expansion, but it further served the Kaiser's purpose by forcing Austria into war with Serbia, thereby making Austria responsible, in the eyes of the world, for launching the conflict which the Kaiser had planned.

There has never been any conclusive proof, remember, that the Serbs were responsible for Ferdinand's assasination. Not that there is anything in their history which would lead one to believe that they would balk at that method of removing an enemy, but, regarded from a political standpoint, it would have been the most unintelligent and short-sighted thing they could possibly have done. Nor are the Serbs and the Pan-Germans the only ones to whom the crime might logically be traced. Ferdinand, remember, had many enemies within the borders of his own country. The Austrian anticlericals hated and distrusted him because he surrounded himself by Jesuit advisers and because he was believed to be unduly under the influence of the Church of Rome. He was equally unpopular with a large and powerful element of the Hungarians, who foresaw a serious diminution of their influence in the affairs of the monarchy should the Archduke succeed in realizing his dream of a Triple Kingdom composed of Austria, Hungary and the Southern Slavs.

Strange indeed are the changes which have been brought about by the greatest conflict. Ferdinand, descendant of a long line of princes, kings and emperors, has passed round that dark corner whence no man returns, but his ambitious dreams of a triple kingdom which would include the Southern Slavs have survived him, though in a somewhat modified form. But he who sits on the throne of the new kingdom, and who rules to-day over a great portion of the former dominions of the Hapsburgs, instead of being a scion of the Imperial House of Austria, is the great-grandson of a Serbian blacksmith.

Owing to the ill-health and advanced age of King Peter of Serbia, his second son, Alexander, is Prince-Regent of the Kingdom of the Serbs, Croats and Slovenes. Prince Alexander, a slender, dark-complexioned man with characteristically Slav features, was educated in Vienna and is said to be an excellent soldier. He is extremely democratic, simple in manner, a student, a hard worker, and devoted to the best interests of his people. Though he is an accomplished horseman, a daring, even reckless motorist, and an excellent shot, he is probably the loneliest man in his kingdom, for he has no close associates of his own age, being surrounded by elderly and serious-minded advisers; his aged father is in a sanitarium, his scapegrace elder brother lives in Paris, and his sister, a Russian grand duchess, makes her home on the Riviera. Though old beyond his years and visibly burdened by the responsibilities of his difficult position, he possesses a peculiarly winning manner and is immensely popular with his soldiers, whose hardships he shared throughout the war. Though he enjoys no great measure of popularity among his new Croat and Slovene subjects, who might be expected to regard any Serb ruler with a certain degree of jealousy and suspicion, he has unquestionably won their profound respect. It is a difficult and trying position which this young man occupies, and it is not made any easier for him, I imagine, by the knowledge that, should he make a false step, should he arouse the enmity of certain of the powerful factions which surround him, the fate of his predecessor and namesake, King Alexander, might quite conceivably befall him.

I have been asked if, in my opinion, the peoples composing the new state of Jugoslavia will stick together. If there could be effected a confederation, modeled on that of Switzerland or the United States, in which the component states would have equal representation, with the executive power vested in a Federal Council, as in Switzerland, then I believe that Jugoslavia would develop into a stable and prosperous nation. But I very much doubt if the Croats, the Slovenes, the Bosnians and the Montenegrins will willingly consent to a permanent arrangement whereby the new nation is placed under a Serbian dynasty, no matter how complete are the safeguards afforded by the constitution or how conscientious and fair-minded the sovereign himself may be. No one questions the ability or the honesty of purpose of Prince Alexander, but the non-Serb elements feel, and not wholly without justification, that a Serbian prince on the throne means Serbian politicians in places of authority, thereby giving Serbia a disproportionate share of authority in the government of Jugoslavia, as Prussia had in the government of the German Empire.

Already there have been manifestations of friction between the Serbs and the Croats and between the Serbs and the Slovenes, to say nothing of the open hostility which exists between the Serbs and certain Montenegrin factions, to which I have alluded in a preceding chapter. It should be remembered that the Croats and Slovenes, though members of the great family of Southern Slavs, have by no means as much in common with their Serb kinsmen as is generally believed. Croatia and Slovenia have both educated and wealthy classes. Serbia, on the contrary, has a very small educated class and practically no wealthy class, it being said that there is not a millionaire in the country. Slovenia and Croatia each have their aristocracies, with titles and estates and traditions; Serbia's population is wholly composed of peasants, or of business and professional men who come from peasant stock. As a result of the large sums which were spent on public instruction in Croatia and Slovenia under Austrian rule, only a comparatively small proportion of the population is illiterate. But in Serbia public education is still in a regrettably backward state, the latest figures available showing that less than seventeen per cent. of the population can read and write, a condition which, I doubt not, will rapidly improve with the reestablishment of peace. Laibach (now known as Lubiana), the chief city of Croatia, Agram, in Slovenia, and Serajevo, the capital of Bosnia, have long been known as education centers, possessing a culture and educational facilities of which far larger cities would have reason to be proud. But Belgrade, having been, as it were, on the frontier of European civilization, has been compelled to concentrate its energies and its resources on commerce and the national defense. The attitude of the people of Agram toward the less sophisticated and cultured Serbs might be compared to that of an educated Bostonian toward an Arizona ranchman—a worthy, industrious fellow, no doubt, but rather lacking in culture and refinement. The truth of the matter is that the Croats and the Slovenes, though only too glad to escape the Allies' wrath by claiming kinship with the Serbs and taking refuge under the banner of Jugoslavia, at heart consider themselves immeasurably superior to their southern kinsmen, whose political dictation, now that the storm has passed, they are beginning to resent.

The first impression which the Serb makes upon a stranger is rarely a favorable one. As an American diplomat, who is a sincere friend of Serbia, remarked to me, "The Serb has neither manner nor manners. The visitor always sees his worst side while his best side remains hidden. He never puts his best foot forward."

A certain sullen defiance of public opinion is, it has sometimes seemed to me, a characteristic of the Serb. He gives one the impression of constantly carrying a chip on his shoulder and daring any one to knock it off. He is always eager for an argument, but, like so many argumentative persons, it is almost impossible to convince him that he is in the wrong. The slightest opposition often drives him into an almost childlike rage and if things go against him he is apt to charge his opponent with insincerity or prejudice. He can see things only one way, *his* way and he resents criticism so violently that it is seldom wise to argue with him.

Though the Serb, when afforded opportunities for education, usually shows great brilliancy as a student and often climbs high in his chosen profession, he all too frequently lacks the mental poise and the power of restraining his passions which are the heritage of those peoples who have been educated for generations.

In Serbia, as in the other Balkan states, it is the peasants who form the most substantial and likeable element of the population. The Serbian peasant is simple, kindly, honest, and hospitable, and, though he could not be described with strict truthfulness as a hard worker, his wife invariably is. Although, like most primitive peoples, he is suspicious of strangers, once he is assured that they are friends there is no sacrifice that he will not make for their comfort, going cold and hungry, if necessary, in order that they may have his blanket and his food. He is one of the very best soldiers in Europe, somewhat careless in dress, drill and discipline, perhaps, but a good shot, a tireless marcher, inured to every form of hardship, and invariably cheerful and uncomplaining. Perhaps it is his instinctive love of soldiering which makes him so reluctant to lay down the rifle and take up the hoe. He has fought three victorious wars in rapid succession and he has come to believe that his metier is fighting. In this he is tacitly encouraged by France, who sees in an armed and ready-to-fight-at-the-drop-of-the-hat Jugoslavia a counterbalance to Italian ambitions in the Balkans.

Though there are irresponsible elements in both Jugoslavia and Italy who talk lightly of war, I am convinced that the great bulk of the population in both countries realize that such a war would be the height of shortsightedness and folly. Throughout the Fiume and Dalmatian crises precipitated by d'Annunzio, Jugoslavia behaved with exemplary patience, dignity and discretion. Let her future foreign relations continue to be characterized by such self-control; let her turn her energies to developing the vast territories to which she has so unexpectedly fallen heir; let her take immediate steps toward inaugurating systems of transportation, public instruction and sanitation; let her waste no time in ridding herself of her jingo politicians and officers—let Jugoslavia do these things and her future will take care of itself. She is a young country, remember. Let us be charitable in judging her.

FOOTNOTES:

Portions of this sketch of the Albanians are drawn from an article which I wrote some years ago for *The Independent*. E.A.P.